Positive Dog Training

Third Edition
by Pamela Dennison

ALPHA

A member of Penguin Group (USA) Inc.

ALPHA BOOKS

Published by the Penguin Group

Penguin Group (USA) Inc., 375 Hudson Street, New York, New York 10014, USA

Penguin Group (Canada), 90 Eglinton Avenue East, Suite 700, Toronto, Ontario M4P 2Y3, Canada (a division of Pearson Penguin Canada Inc.)

Penguin Books Ltd., 80 Strand, London WC2R 0RL, England

Penguin Ireland, 25 St. Stephen's Green, Dublin 2, Ireland (a division of Penguin Books Ltd.)

Penguin Group (Australia), 250 Camberwell Road, Camberwell, Victoria 3124, Australia (a division of Pearson Australia Group Pty. Ltd.)

Penguin Books India Pvt. Ltd., 11 Community Centre, Panchsheel Park, New Delhi—110 017, India

Penguin Group (NZ), 67 Apollo Drive, Rosedale, North Shore, Auckland 1311, New Zealand (a division of Pearson New Zealand Ltd.)

Penguin Books (South Africa) (Pty.) Ltd., 24 Sturdee Avenue, Rosebank, Johannesburg 2196, South Africa

Penguin Books Ltd., Registered Offices: 80 Strand, London WC2R 0RL, England

Copyright © 2011 by Pamela Dennison

International Standard Book Number: 978-1-61564-066-9
Library of Congress Catalog Card Number: 2010910469

13   12   11   8   7   6   5   4   3   2

Interpretation of the printing code: The rightmost number of the first series of numbers is the year of the book's printing; the rightmost number of the second series of numbers is the number of the book's printing. For example, a printing code of 11-1 shows that the first printing occurred in 2011.

Printed in the United States of America

Note: This publication contains the opinions and ideas of its author. It is intended to provide helpful and informative material on the subject matter covered. It is sold with the understanding that the author and publisher are not engaged in rendering professional services in the book. If the reader requires personal assistance or advice, a competent professional should be consulted.

The author and publisher specifically disclaim any responsibility for any liability, loss, or risk, personal or otherwise, which is incurred as a consequence, directly or indirectly, of the use and application of any of the contents of this book.

Publisher: *Marie Butler-Knight*
Associate Publisher: *Mike Sanders*
Executive Editor: *Randy Ladenheim-Gil*
Senior Managing Editor: *Billy Fields*
Senior Development Editor: *Phil Kitchel*
Senior Production Editor: *Janette Lynn*
Copy Editor: *Tricia Liebig*

Cover Designer: *Rebecca Batchelor*
Book Designers: *William Thomas, Rebecca Batchelor*
Indexer: *Johnna Vanhoose Dinse*
Layout: *Ayanna Lacey*
Proofreader: *Laura Caddell*

To U-CD Commander Cody's Great Escape, CGC, A-CD, CDX, NJC, October 18, 1992–June 6, 2005, my "crossover" dog: Sorry it took so long for me to find positive training, and thank you for being such a patient dog.

Contents

Foreword

After 25 years of reading, researching, and applying animal training to an assortment of finned, flippered, feathered, and furred critters—from whales to walruses, from dolphins to dogs—I can confidently state that it's finally here: a succinct guide to dog training that explains the often-confusing and complex science of animal learning in simple terms.

Dogs are remarkable animals capable of learning a variety of complex behaviors if owners commit a little time each day and train in small steps using patience and understanding. When they are rewarded for each of these small steps, dogs can learn as fast as dolphins, chimpanzees, or even killer whales. For new pet owners, however, training always seems easiest right before they actually bring the new dog home to live. How hard could it be to teach a "sit," or to walk calmly on a leash, or basic potty training? That is until you realize that the wet spot on the rug is not water, that the neighbors really don't appreciate barking at 2:00 A.M., and that a "let's go" is supposed to cue your new pet to walk forward and not to go in reverse. As we often learn, what seems simple can get awfully complicated.

Pam Dennison has been a tireless advocate for positive, productive, and enriching training methods, most of which she has outlined in this guide. As a dog-training instructor and award-winning obedience trainer, Pam has patiently guided dog owners so that they might better understand the process of reducing unwanted behavior in a positive and productive way, while maintaining a trusting relationship with their pet. At the same time, she also teaches dog owners how to shape new behaviors such as basic obedience, potty training, and proper socialization with children. Advanced trainers have also benefited from Pam's expertise, especially in competition obedience training, where her skills are most obvious.

But most notably, she has enough confidence in her personal-training knowledge and applied skills to take on some extreme behavior challenges using the same techniques outlined in the following pages. The results have been remarkable. Her success with a highly aggressive Border Collie named Shadow has been a shining example of training excellence that quite literally changed Shadow's life. The training that Shadow received transformed him from a severely aggressive and reactive animal to a well-trained and well-mannered pet. Even more remarkable, Shadow is now competing in registered trials and doing excellent!

The rewards of dog ownership become evident when animals are taught behaviors that help them live comfortably and confidently in the household. The relationship between a family and their pet is further strengthened when fascinating behaviors are trained that highlight their pet's intelligence and personality. Finally, true miracles are accomplished when owners learn how to change behaviors in a way that positively impacts the quality of life for animals challenged with overcoming fear, anxiety, phobias, and aggression. In a very practical way, this guide addresses many of these areas and has synthesized the multitude of training techniques into a helpful tool, complete with real examples, entertaining stories, and valuable training exercises. The rest is up to you. Stay positive and keep the training fun!

—Ted Turner, animal behaviorist

Introduction

Thank you for choosing to train your best friend using purely positive techniques! Positive training has been proven by behavioral psychologists to be the most effective way to train any behavior. As you will see, punishment causes toxic side effects and can harm your relationship with your dog. There are many, many ways to let your dog know that you don't like his behavior without punishing or yelling at him.

When I started training, I went to a "traditional" punishment-based training class. After a while, I was seeing a decrease of "good" behaviors and an increase of "bad" behaviors with my dogs. They started to hate training and I was angry all of the time.

I was at a standstill in my training for competition because the only advice given in traditional training was to use more and harsher punishment. This made no sense to me and I went on a learning quest, found positive training, "crossed over," and started my business, Positive Motivation Dog Training, in 1996.

For those of you who have trained a dog using traditional methods, it may take a while for you to get the hang of not punishing your dog, but you will see faster results and then be hooked, just like I was!

How to Use This Book

In this book, you'll find everything you need to know about positive training, from where it all began in the laboratory to how to successfully use positive methods in your own home with your own dog.

Part 1, Positively Amazing, teaches you the science behind the method, where it all came from, common myths of positive training, and what happens if you use punishment.

Part 2, How Dogs Learn and Communicate, covers how dogs learn, the signals dogs give us, and how we can use them for better training. This part also gets you started on teaching your dog her name, to look at you adoringly at all times, and the very first steps to teaching the "Come" command.

Part 3, Positive Training in Action, teaches you how to teach your dog sit, down, door etiquette, loose-leash walking, and stays. In addition, you will learn how to use reinforcement schedules properly and how to utilize things that the dog already likes as rewards for training. And you'll learn answers to that age-old question: how to respond in a positive way if your dog makes a mistake.

Part 4, Dogs and Your Lifestyle, discusses how to add a new dog to your household, how to help your dogs and kids get along, and how to deal with "bad" behaviors such as jumping, biting, attention deficit disorder in dogs, stealing, and resource guarding. In addition, this part teaches you how to train while holding down a full-time job and what other options are open for you and your dog once you master basic training; it also includes how to train for the Canine Good Citizen certificate.

Extras

Check out the sidebars throughout the book. They're packed full of fun and informative facts:

> **DOGGIE DATA**
>
> Case studies of real dogs and people and interesting facts you won't want to miss.

> **CANINE CAVEATS**
>
> You'll find warnings here. Ignore at your own risk.

> **POOCH POINTERS**
>
> Tips to help make you a better trainer.

> **MUTTLEY MEANINGS**
>
> Definitions for technical terms made simple.

Acknowledgments

My undying gratitude goes to my agent Jacky Sachs and her "bad" dog Roscoe; for without him, we never would have met and this book never would have been written. Many millions of thanks to Jane Killion for her incredible patience and dozens of phone calls ("Jane, will you pick my brain for me?") helping me coalesce my thoughts for this book. To my assistant, Meg Irizarry, for her help in finding great websites.

To my circle of "doggie friends," Ted Turner, Cynthia and John Palmer, Jan and Brian Guz, Patty Ruzzo, and Carolyn Wilki, for teaching me so much on the road to positive methods. And for those people who don't even know me, but who had a major impact on my life: Leslie Nelson, Bob Bailey, and Turid Rugaas.

And to the dogs—mine: Cody, Beau, Shadow, and Mollie, and others who have played a role in this book and in my continuing education: Boomer, Sergeant, Mia, Sasha, Bo, Biscuit, Needle, Jazz, Primo, Satch, Ruby, Cherry, Nicky, Dixie, Sirius, Beauty, Tripper, Lucas, and more, many of whom are disguised in this book.

To my mother, Zelda Gross, who said, "Of course you can do it."

Trademarks

All terms mentioned in this book that are known to be or are suspected of being trademarks or service marks have been appropriately capitalized. Alpha Books and Penguin Group (USA) Inc. cannot attest to the accuracy of this information. Use of a term in this book should not be regarded as affecting the validity of any trademark or service mark.

Positively Amazing

I hope to lead you on the most exciting adventure of your life as a dog owner. Part 1 discusses the science behind the method of positive training, who uses positive training and why, the most common myths about positive training, and what happens (proven by science) if you use punishment-based methods to train your dog.

Training your dog should be fun, awesome, and enlightening for both you and your dog. Dog ownership does take time, brain power (not muscle power), and money, but the benefits are enormous in terms of the relationship you will have with your chosen "best friend." If you don't have time to train your dog, get a stuffed animal instead.

Positive Training Fundamentals

In This Chapter

- Discovering the basic principles and rules of positive training
- Being positive is easier and faster than punishment
- Learning that positive methods create no bad side effects
- Teaching your dog in small, successful steps

Positive training is precise manipulation of favorable consequences (good stuff, such as food and toys) to get your dog to perform the behaviors you want. The cool thing is data from the science of behavioral psychology proves that positive training is successful under the most rigorous conditions, so the methodology in this book is not just "one person's opinion."

"Positive" doesn't equal "permissive." My dogs are subject to strict rules and regulations around the house and proper manners when we're away from home. I never use physical or verbal punishment on my dogs. I don't rule by force and my dogs don't rule the roost. I do, however, have some of the best-trained dogs around and have earned multiple titles in multiple dog sports. My dogs are a pleasure to live with—are yours?

If you are so inclined, you can certainly use old-fashioned elbow grease and spend many hours to clean your oven, because that's how your mother used to do it; or you can use an oven cleaner, make your job easier, and then go out and have fun.

You can undoubtedly train your dog using traditional techniques, utilizing punishment, physical manipulation, and intimidation, because that's the way (you think) everyone trains dogs; or you can use positive methods—and then go out and have fun! And because you now have a well-trained dog, you might actually be able to take him with you.

What Is This Clicker Thing?

Clicker training is one facet of positive training that uses a signal to tell the dog that he did something right. A clicker is simply a marker signal—a specific sound that marks the correct behavior the instant the dog performs it. You make the sound of the click valuable by associating food with the noise. The clicker itself is a small plastic box with a metal tongue that creates a "click" sound when pressed. You can find them in most large pet and dog-equipment stores.

Clicker training (positive training and clicker training are used interchangeably in this book) teaches dogs to think and to use the wonderful, creative brains they have. It also teaches them that they do have some control, in a way that brings their own propensities into the training process. When you start training using the clicker, you'll see that your dog isn't working for the food—he's working to get you to click.

The Clicker Helps Your Timing, Too!

The clicker also imparts valuable information to the trainer. When you try to mark the behavior with words, such as the ever-popular "good dog," it's hard to tell whether or not you're late in marking the behavior.

With the clicker, you can easily tell when you're late, which will help you fix your timing. If you have been continuously late with your verbal "good dog," then you can pretty much assume that your dog is confused and probably not getting it. You then wrongly think that your dog is stupid when, in fact, you were the one who wasn't clear. Positive training takes the onus off your dog and puts it squarely where it belongs—on you. The dog is never wrong. Really. We're the teachers. We're the ones in the driver's seat.

A few correct repetitions do not a learned behavior make. And if the dog performs a wrong behavior, so what? We all make mistakes or do stupid things—even when we know better. I'm allergic to certain foods, but I eat them anyway. And I sometimes say stupid things (insert foot in mouth).

Step-by-step instructions for using a clicker for teaching specific behaviors are addressed in Chapters 9, 10, and 11.

A Short Bit of History

Ivan Pavlov (1849–1936) is the man who gave us Pavlovian conditioning, also called classical conditioning. You remember Pavlov with the dog, the bell, and the drool? Pavlov learned through his research that if he paired a neutral stimulus (a bell—something that previously had no meaning for the dog) with meat powder, after a few repetitions, the dog would drool upon hearing the bell.

So why is this important? Associations are the first steps to learning anything. To bring this closer to home, let's say on your first ever day of school, you hear a bell. You have no idea what it means, but you are shepherded into the lunchroom. Pretty soon, when you hear the bell, your stomach may start to growl, or if you are really hungry that day, you may start to salivate. What you have done is associate the sound of the bell (which had no meaning for you before) with a whole new implication—lunchtime!

Who Let the Cat Out of the Box?

B. F. Skinner (1904–1990) was a forerunner in the study of operant conditioning, secondary reinforcers, and ratios of reinforcement. (For more information, see Chapters 4 and 8.) He discovered that changes in behavior are a result of the individual's response (observable behavior) to the events happening in the environment. Learning is the outcome of change in observable behaviors.

And this is critical because? Observable behavior is key here because if you can't observe a change in behavior (for better or worse), then you can't know or assume that learning has occurred. You can't read your dog's mind, but you can observe her behavior.

Operant conditioning is covered in more depth in Chapter 4.

Positive Policies: The Three Laws of Learning

There are a few simple rules for using positive methods. I know they may sound too simplistic to really be effective. In addition, when you start, the routine might seem insurmountable. But after you get the hang of positive training, it will all become more natural and second nature.

Whether you use positive reinforcement or punishment-based methods, the laws of learning remain the same. It doesn't make any difference if you're training a dog, person, cat, or goat. The three basic laws are here:

- Rewarded behavior gets repeated.

- Ignored behavior stops.

- Variable rewards strengthen the behavior when a behavior is in place.

Notice I never said only good behaviors are strengthened. Let's say you continually leave food on the counter and your dog has been rewarded many times for stealing it. So you start keeping your counters spotlessly clean, and after a while your dog stops thinking about jumping up to steal some food. Then you get busy, start forgetting to put the food away, and your dog starts taking food off the counter again. You go back to putting the food away, but because your dog has now been randomly reinforced for jumping on the counter, that behavior will become very strong.

The First Law of Learning

Behavior that is rewarded is most likely to be repeated:

> Your dog mauls you when you come home wearing a clean suit. Because you pay attention to him (either positively or negatively), he will continue to maul you whenever you come home.

You might wonder how negative attention (yelling or hitting) could be rewarding for the dog. If the only time you interact with your dog is to tell him what he did wrong, then he'll continue to do those very behaviors. Sounds pretty stupid doesn't it? But to the dog, being yelled at is preferable to being ignored. It isn't as though I don't punish my dogs, but the punishment consists of ignoring them. Because my attention is so positively reinforcing for my dogs, being ignored sends a very strong message that "Mom isn't happy."

The Second Law of Learning

Behavior that is not reinforced will most likely stop (extinguish):

> You come home, your dog starts to maul you, and you now ignore the dog for about 10 minutes until she relaxes, and then you pay attention to her.

Now when you come home, she will lie down and relax until you come over to greet her.

The Third Law of Learning

After a behavior is established, a variable schedule of reinforcement will make the behavior stronger:

> You come home and are wearing old clothes, so you allow the dog to jump on you, but you continue to ignore the dog when you're wearing a suit.

Guess what? Your dog isn't a fashion critic and will continue to maul you when you come home, because you are variably (sometimes yes and sometimes no) reinforcing the jumping.

Unlike classical conditioning, where a natural, reflexive behavior (such as salivating for food) is associated with a new stimulus (the metronome), *operant conditioning* rewards a partial behavior or a random act that resembles the desired end behavior.

Reinforcing What You Like

You'd be surprised how many people don't know what they want in terms of their dog's behavior. If you don't know what you want, you won't recognize it when you get it! "I just want a good dog" doesn't count. You may want a dog that doesn't pull on the leash or jump on strangers or try to set her own place at the dinner table. Learn to be more specific.

Make a list of the behaviors you observe in your dog now, along with what you'd rather see instead. Here's an example:

Existing Behavior	What You Want Instead
Jumping on strangers	Sitting politely for petting
Pulling on the leash	Walking calmly by my side
Barking at the doorbell	Quiet when doorbell rings
Bucking bronco for grooming	Standing still for grooming
Growling at strangers	Watching strangers calmly

When you identify what you want, you'll be surprised at how often you actually do get these behaviors—even without training. No dog can be "bad" 24 hours a day, 7 days a week. Really. Not even yours. And now you can start reinforcing the "good" behaviors because you know what to look for.

For instance, your dog is rearranging the furniture in nightly "puppy zoomies," where she runs around and around, completely out of control, sliding into furniture and knocking over lamps. Why not reinforce her when she's lying down being quiet? Behavior that is positively rewarded will be repeated. Reward her for lying down, and ignore puppy zoomies. As long as she's getting proper exercise, she'll lie down more often as a result.

Many of the annoying behaviors your dog has can be easily changed and incorporated into your training in many ways. You could turn an annoying behavior into an outlet for some exercise, or a reinforcer for good behavior.

For instance, when Beau was a puppy, he used to steal my shoes and eat them. Rather than do the sensible thing and put my shoes away, I decided to teach him to retrieve them. As he paraded past me with a "neener, neener, neener" look on his face, I clicked and praised him. He dropped the shoe in surprise. I gave him a few treats and encouraged him to bring me the shoe. After repeating this a few times, he actually stopped stealing my shoes and brought me toys instead.

Even if your dog ends up always stealing things and bringing them to you for a treat, it's better than taking those same objects, eating them, and ending up in the emergency vet's office for surgery.

Ignoring What You Don't Like

Easier said than done. Now that you know what you do want, I'm sure you know what you don't want. You can address the unwanted behaviors in a few ways:

- Completely and utterly ignore them—simply walk away, go into another room, or leave the house.
- Redirect the dog to a behavior you can then positively reinforce.
- Manage the situation better by putting the dog in his crate *before* he starts driving you crazy.

> **CANINE CAVEATS**
>
> When you're redirecting the dog to a better behavior, be careful. You don't want to accidentally reinforce the dog for doing the "bad" behavior. For instance, you're busy and can't pay attention to your dog, so he then nips you or bothers you in inappropriate ways. You then redirect to a toy. What has your dog learned? "Bother Mom and Dad and they will play with me."
>
> This is how you should properly handle redirection: Dog is bothering you? Ask for an incompatible behavior—Sits or Downs usually work well for most situations. Count to five while the dog remains in position. *Then* redirect the dog. This way, the dog associates "sit calmly and I get attention," rather than "be annoying and I get attention."

What if you can't watch the dog because you're preparing a sit-down dinner for 50 people and he wants to sample the menu to make sure no one gets poisoned (such a selfless doggie!)? Put him in his crate beforehand with a nice juicy bone, and voilà! Uncle Ben's Instant Good Dog!

Breaking Down Behaviors

The key to training your dog is to help her *experience success without the fear of making mistakes.* This is achieved through *approximation training.* Picture a flip-book, where you flip the pages and it looks like a movie. Whatever behavior you want, make a mental flip-book of it. Then just train each page. The key to success is to know how to break each behavior down into its smallest components so that your dog can understand the behavior. These small successes set her up to be right, thereby keeping her interest, as well as building her confidence.

Breaking behaviors into small segments, rather than lumping big chunks of behaviors together, makes it easier for the dog to understand. You didn't start out with calculus before you knew that 1 + 1 = 2. You owe it to your dog to help her be successful.

> **MUTTLEY MEANINGS**
>
> **Approximations** are breaking behaviors down into small steps that make up a final behavior.

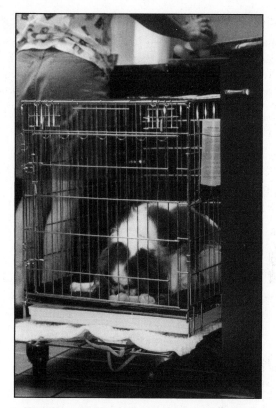

This dog is in his crate, happily chewing a bone.
(Photo by P. Dennison)

If you expect your dog to walk on a loose leash for a mile the first time you put a leash on him, you're setting him up to fail, and setting yourself up to be annoyed. Any behavior, no matter how seemingly easy (to you), can be broken down into very small steps.

Start by teaching the dog to look at you while on leash, then move to one step of loose-leash walking, then two steps, then three, and so on. This breaks the behavior down into manageable and attainable pieces. (In-depth instructions for teaching loose-leash walking are in Chapter 10.)

Communicating so that the dog can understand is the key. Remember when you first learned to tie your shoes? Your mom didn't just tell you to go for it: she probably did it for you a few times, and then showed you how to hold the laces, cross them, make the loops, and so on.

Raising the Criteria with Each Step

Let's look at heeling (see Chapter 10). Start out by reinforcing each step of heeling until your dog is glued to your leg. Then raise your criteria and only reinforce every other step. Then raise your criteria again and reward every third step, and so on. After a while, you'll be able to get longer and longer heeling for less and less rewards.

Your job is to advance behaviors, so don't get too stuck on each step when building a long behavior chain.

> **POOCH POINTERS**
>
> If the behavior being taught is complicated, an even shorter session is called for. Don't be afraid to train the dog for as little as 30 seconds or for just one correct repetition.

The Definition of a Learned Behavior

Many people mistakenly think that a dog who happens to perform a behavior once or twice on cue actually *knows* the cue. You may think that your dog is just being stubborn or stupid, but in reality he is just undertrained. The dog doesn't know it yet because he has not experienced enough correct repetitions in enough varied situations. Dogs are notoriously poor generalizers—just because your dog knows the behavior at home, this does not mean that he will know it elsewhere. What your dog learns in the kitchen, stays in the kitchen!

I like to use behavioral psychology's definition of a learned behavior: "A learned behavior is one that occurs correctly in at least 8 out of 10 tries, out of 10 trials." If your dog cannot perform a behavior correctly 80 out of 100 times, then she hasn't learned it yet. It's that simple. I would like to add my own addendum to that definition— "and in at least 15 new and different locations with varying levels of distraction." If this sounds daunting, take heart! The more novel environments and distractions you include in your training, the quicker your dog will learn to generalize.

Keeping Sessions Short and Successful

Continuous failure is a poor teacher. It can create a frustrated, aggressive, or quitter animal. The optimum sessions are three to five minutes, three to five times per day, working on only two or three behaviors each time.

Fixing Bad Behaviors by Reinforcing Good Ones

Reinforce your dog for having four paws on the floor rather than jumping. Reinforce the dog for walking on a loose leash rather than pulling. Reinforce the dog for having a toy in her mouth rather than your arm. By focusing on the good stuff, the bad stuff usually goes away with very little extra training.

Watching Your Timing

Timing is everything. Improper timing using positive methods slows down learning. Improper timing using punishment methods constitutes abuse. Don't get me wrong—bad timing using positive methods can create more bad behaviors, but these are easy to fix when you fix your timing.

CANINE CAVEATS

A dog can see continual repetitions of behaviors (drilling) as a form of punishment. Even if the behavior is correct each time, it can get tedious. You want learning to be fun for your dog, not boring.

My rule of thumb is this: if the dog does something great, reinforce (or click and then reinforce if the dog is far away) within a half second. If the dog does something less than desirable, wait a full 5 to 10 seconds after he stops doing the unwanted behavior, redirect to a better behavior, and then reinforce.

The Positives of Positive Training

Positive training is easy on the dogs, it increases their love of learning (and of you), it gives them a better quality of life, and overall it helps them lead happier lives.

On the other hand, positive training is hard on the trainer (at first) because you have to use your brain (ouch!). It is much easier to yell, scold, spank, hit, and get angry than it is to think, "What did *I* do to train my dog to act this way and what can I do to get him to stop?"

Keep Strong Emotions Out of Training

When our flawed human emotions come into play, our functional intelligence disappears. It's hard to stop and reflect when we're emotionally charged. When you can do that, however, training becomes easier and much more fun for you and your dog.

Becoming more patient just takes practice and the sincere knowledge that losing your temper does nothing to teach the dog anything. In fact, getting angry is more harmful than helpful—to both of you.

A Gentler Approach Is More Effective

Positive training is more effective for training any species in any behavior that they're physically capable of doing. You might say, "But how can *not* punishing my dog actually be more effective? I *have* to tell her what she did wrong."

My motto is, if you aren't ignoring the dog (for "bad" behavior), then you're reinforcing it.

If you pay attention to only "good" behaviors, then your dog will continue to do those things that bring her your attention. If you pay attention to both "good" *and* "bad" behaviors, then you're confusing the heck out of your dog! Because both are being reinforced, the dog will continue to do both.

Or, at the very least, you're nagging the dog with machine-gun Sits ("sitsitsitsitsitsit") or not giving the dog any direction other than

"NO!", until she just shuts you out completely. Think about when you're learning something new. How would you feel if every time you goofed, the teacher kept saying "Wrong!" It would get really frustrating, to say the least, and you'd probably end up disliking the teacher or the subject.

> **POOCH POINTERS**
>
> You can, in fact, "punish" your dog—and positive trainers do punish dogs, but not in the traditional sense of the word. Trainers may withhold a reinforcer, or access to fun, or (horror of horrors) ignore the dog for a few seconds! Omigod! Call out the humane society!

The very idea that a dog escapes punishment or gets away with something is appalling for some people. It's hard for us to comprehend how an animal can actually learn better without it, but it works because attention is the thing a dog craves most (and humans, too). In fact, if you physically or verbally punish the dog, you run a very high risk of creating much worse behaviors than the ones you started with.

Say that your teacher asks a question and you think you know the response. You raise your hand enthusiastically, blurt out your answer, and oops, you get it wrong. You get smacked down for guessing incorrectly. The next time a question is asked, you'll sit on your hands and avert your eyes to avoid being called on. The rest of the class who witnessed your punishment will also be sitting on their hands.

Now for the flip side. The teacher walks in with a *huge* jar of candy and announces that anyone who attempts to answer a question will get a piece of candy. The students who give correct answers will get a whole *handful* of candy. More students will try harder, pay closer attention to the lesson, and do their homework more thoroughly—and happily. This system—positive reinforcement—encourages the students to *think!*

It's more effective to teach dogs' minds rather than manipulate their bodies. You should work *with*, rather than against, your dog during training sessions. And you should help inexperienced dogs rather than reprimand them.

It's Just Faster

Positively trained dogs—those who are not punished—will freely offer behaviors in an effort to elicit a good response from their trainers, will grasp information more quickly, and will be able to learn more advanced behaviors at a much earlier age than most other training methods encourage. Behaviors that take months or years to correct using punishment-based methods now take weeks, days, hours, or even minutes to teach using positive methods.

> **DOGGIE DATA**
>
> Leanne wanted to teach her dog Toby to lie down on his bed while Leanne was eating dinner, instead of mauling her and incessantly begging for food. Using the clicker and a small handful of treats, we taught Toby, in less than five minutes, to go to his bed when Leanne was eating.

No Bad Side Effects

You may sometimes hear the phrase "balanced training." There's nothing magical about balanced trainers; it's just a nifty catch phrase. It means that the trainer uses traditional, force-based techniques, as well as positive reinforcement when the dog is correct.

This is just confusing to the dog and makes him less likely to offer behaviors. This type of training teaches the dog to possibly work for you to avoid punishment, but it does not teach the dog to *willingly* work for you. Other dogs may just shut down from the punishment and end up doing absolutely nothing.

If you punish your dog for "bad" behaviors, you risk creating aggression, fear, anxiety, *learned helplessness*, or a stubborn or stupid dog. Sure, you may immediately suppress the "bad" behavior, but that doesn't mean that the "bad" behavior is gone forever.

- Punish your dog for eating your socks, and he might start chewing on the wallpaper instead.

- Punish your dog for jumping and he might become so afraid of people that he bites instead of jumping.

- Punish your dog for doing a behavior wrong and he might become neurotic about trying again.

 MUTTLEY MEANINGS

Learned helplessness occurs when the dog (or human) just shuts down because nothing she does is ever right, so she just gives up.

Pop Quiz

1. How many times did you notice that you used the word "no"?

2. How many times did you catch your dog doing something *right*? Did you reinforce for that "good" behavior?

3. How many times did you inadvertently reinforce your dog for doing something "bad"? (Reinforcements include yelling, saying "no," talking to the dog, comforting the dog, and so on.)

4. Have you made the list of the behaviors you'd *rather* have your dog do?

5. What is an approximation?

6. What is the definition of a learned behavior?

The true benefit of positive training is the trust that the dog learns. The trust that says she can offer behaviors without fear of recrimination. The trust that says you will not hurt her. We owe it to our dogs to keep that trust.

The Least You Need to Know

- The fundamentals of positive training include reinforcing good behavior, ignoring bad behavior, breaking down the desired behavior into small steps, and watching your timing.
- Be sure you know what behaviors you want from your dog.
- Redirect your dog, or better yet, stop "bad" behaviors before they start.
- Positive training is better than negative training because it's easier, more effective, faster, has no bad side effects, and helps you and your dog have a happier relationship.
- The laws of learning, as with gravity, are always in effect.

Positive Training Myths Dispelled

In This Chapter

- Easy, fad-free training
- Your dog always has a choice about how to behave
- The tortoise or the hare—which is faster?
- Positive training: dealing with barking and aggression the most effective way

Myths such as the ones that follow, spring up primarily because of the general lack of understanding of classical and operant conditioning and positive training. Here are my favorite responses to these misconceptions. It's hard to change old habits and old mindsets; however, you'll see that positive training isn't so difficult after all. Going against the "old school" may be difficult at times, but will be worth it when you achieve a wonderful relationship with your dog.

It's Not Just the Latest Craze, and It's Easy to Learn

You're sure to hear discouraging comments like these from your friends or other dog trainers: positive clicker training is a fad or gimmick, or the principles are too hard to learn and to understand.

Myth #1: The Clicker Is a Fad or Gimmick

Actually, using a conditioned reinforcer (such as a clicker) is a training method based on sound, scientifically proven, psychological principles, as discussed in Chapter 1. Skinner and others have conducted extensive research on the effectiveness of conditioned reinforcers in training.

As with anything, if you use the clicker or positive training improperly, it won't work. Give your dog a treat for barking, "to shut him up," and he'll continue to bark. I've seen ill-informed trainers use the clicker as a recall signal, as a sound with no meaning (in other words, no treat follows the sound), or just randomly, with no thought of what they were actually reinforcing. Use it incorrectly and you can easily create aggression, fear, and avoidance.

Myth #2: The Principles Are Too Difficult

This is absolutely not true. Although positive training involves a lot of technical information, you don't have to be thoroughly versed to understand how it works.

It's easy, however, to become a "behavior junkie," because learning how dogs learn is so fascinating. Many people come to me saying, "I just want a dog that doesn't jump or pull," and then become so mesmerized that they stay to learn more.

CANINE CAVEATS

Without knowing the science behind the method, it's easy to fall back into the punishment mode of training, especially when you become impatient or frustrated by your dog's behavior.

After you know the "whys" of behavior, it's easy to fix problem behaviors—and better yet, to stop them before they start.

Helping Your Dog Make the *Right* Choices

Additional things you may hear from tradition-based trainers: training using positive reinforcement/clickers takes much longer than traditional punishment-based training, and a dog should never be given a choice.

In this age of more things to do in less time, the word "faster" may be a real draw for us. However, when building a relationship, it takes as long as it takes. You can't rush a bond—with dogs or with other people. You certainly can't build that rapport using punishment.

We all make choices in our lives. Sometimes we choose incorrectly. That is called a mistake. Dogs and people trained using positive methods sometimes make the wrong choices, as do dogs and people trained using punishment methods. Did you get beaten the last time you goofed? If your dog makes a mistake, lighten up!

Myth #3: Positive Reinforcement Takes Too Long

Actually, positive methods have been proven to speed up learning. In the beginning stages, it seems to take longer only because you may have to wait a whole 5 or 10 seconds (!) for the dog to think, rather than forcing the dog into position.

However, after you and your dog catch on, clicker training leads to much faster results. (Dogs usually catch on faster than humans.) Dogs very quickly learn to perform the desired behaviors to make you click! In addition, behaviors learned through positive reinforcement and positive associations tend to stay with the dog for the rest of her life.

I had a mother come to me a few years ago with an adorable puppy and a very bratty 10-year-old boy. He was obnoxious toward his mother as well as to me. While he was taking the puppy for a potty walk, I asked Mom what was up with her son. She explained that there was a great age difference between this boy and the next oldest sibling, and that he was acting this way for attention.

I recommended that she treat him just as she would her puppy. If he was obnoxious, she was to turn around and leave the room. If he was appropriate, she was to reinforce him in any way that made sense for a 10-year-old boy. The following week, he was a model of decorum and turned out to be quite bright and nice. During a break, when he was out of the room, I asked her, "Wow! What a difference! What did you do?" Her reply, "I did exactly what you told me to do and he is now correcting himself and apologizing if he forgets and he talks back." So in just one week of using positive methods, she was able to teach her son to behave properly, when for many years, all of the yelling yielded even more impolite behaviors.

Myth #4: Never Give a Dog a Choice

Clicker trainers set up the situation so that their dogs make the desired choices. Dogs always have behavioral choices, even when they're trained with aversives (corrections and/or punishment). To think they don't is an illusion.

I've seen dogs make mistakes regardless of whether they're trained using punishment *or* positive reinforcement. I've also seen people make mistakes—sometimes the same ones over and over again.

Let's Use Our Brains!

You may also hear that positive/clicker training is too difficult because you must always have a clicker with you, and positively trained dogs won't work without food.

Many people think that when you start using a clicker, you must use one for the rest of your life—and you will have to surgically connect one to your hand. If you use the clicker properly, you will be using it only in the beginning, teaching stages of each behavior, and then weaning off of it.

Some trainers out there still believe that dogs should work because they love us and we should not have to "bribe" them with food. I believe that while there may be some dogs somewhere who do things because they "love" us, it's rare. Eventually, if you build a strong relationship with your dog, he may someday just want to work out of the sheer joy of doing things with you. I don't believe in bribing a dog—I believe in reinforcing a dog for correct behavior—a paycheck, if you will. After all, most of us don't work for free.

Myth #5: Always Have the Clicker with You

Although most clicker trainers would probably admit to having clickers stashed everywhere (I personally found 15 clickers in my purse the last time I cleaned it out), they're not necessary every time you work with your dog.

The clicker is used mostly when teaching a new behavior in the beginning stages. You can phase it out once (too many "whens" have been added) the behavior is well learned. Thus, it is very important to make sure that certain words become secondary reinforcers. I use the words "yes" and "that's right" as my "click words." Sometimes it just isn't logical or practical to be holding food, clicker, toys, and the leash. Use these words not as praise, but as a marker signal followed by a reward, just as you would reward after a click.

Myth #6: Clicker-Trained Dogs Won't Work Without Food

I could counter that by saying that punishment-trained dogs won't work without punishment. In the beginning stages of training, I recommend that you use food liberally. Many times, the dogs have no real positive connection with their owners, and food helps to jump-start that connection.

However, a good positive/clicker trainer learns how to go from *continuous* to *variable schedules of reinforcement* and to use other types of reinforcers. Punishment-based trainers often say to me, "Well, you can't bring a clicker into the obedience ring." My reply is, "Well, you can't bring a prong or shock collar into the ring, either."

> **MUTTLEY MEANINGS**
>
> If you give your dog a treat each and every time he does a correct behavior, you're following a **continuous schedule of reinforcement.** If sometimes you give the dog a treat for a correct behavior and sometimes you don't, then you're following a **variable schedule of reinforcement.**

Food is sometimes easier to deliver and doesn't take much thought—get a behavior right, get a cookie. But if you use *only* food as reinforcement, the naysayers will be right—your dog will work only for food. Using other types of reinforcers, such as petting, play, or silly games, takes more thought and planning, but the benefits are enormous (see Chapter 8).

I used to be quite lazy about using reinforcers other than food. One of my dogs was consistently getting nonqualifying scores in competition obedience. I sat back and thought very hard about my training. Aha! The instant I started using toys, all kinds of play, and even silly pet tricks as reinforcers, he started not only qualifying, but getting very high scores as well.

Like the Dependable Maytag Repair Man

Many people believe that behaviors taught using positive methods aren't as reliable as behaviors taught using force.

Myth #7: Force Works Better

Although a dog's desire to avoid pain is strong, the desire to gain pleasant consequences is stronger. Think about the last time you got a speeding ticket—did it stop you from speeding? Much of your dog's behavior is based on what's more reinforcing for her to do.

> **POOCH POINTERS**
>
> Reliability is the bane of all dog trainers, whether or not you compete in the show ring. None of us is 100 percent reliable in everything, and neither are our dogs. Use your head. Don't let your dog off the leash to run rampant in the neighborhood and expect her to come when called.

Let's say you're stopped by the police each time you're not speeding and are rewarded with $100. Every day for a week, you're stopped two or three times per day and handed $100. Then the police go to a random schedule of reinforcement. Now you get stopped only one or two times per day and only three or five times per week. Sometimes you get verbally praised, sometimes you're handed dinner tickets to your favorite restaurant, and sometimes you get the $100.

Once in a while you get pulled over and handed $1,000. Would you ever speed again? I sure wouldn't. I would take that money and run out and buy a van with cruise control because I wouldn't want to miss the chance of possibly getting the rewards! In the same respect, after a dog has learned something (good or bad), he tends to repeat that behavior over and over. Behaviors learned through force tend to fall apart when the dog is under stress. But behaviors learned in pleasant circumstances with positive consequences are less likely to fall apart under pressure.

Myth #8: Positive Training Isn't Effective with Barking or Aggression

Dogs trained using a clicker can be easily taught alternative behaviors to replace the unwanted ones. Trainers using positive principles often devise very creative ways to change undesirable behaviors such as barking and aggression. I've personally used positive training to solve a number of serious behavioral and aggression problems.

I've seen dogs barking in crates. I've seen owners kick the crate, yell at the dog, take the dog out of the crate when they can't stand it anymore or if it becomes an embarrassment, and otherwise reinforce the dog for barking in the crate.

I've seen owners put collars on their dogs that deliver an electric shock or a spray of citronella to get them to stop barking. After a few zaps with the shock collar or some sprays with the citronella collar, they hang the collar on the crate and say, "See? The dog is now not barking." True, but take the collar away and the dog starts barking again because now the threat of punishment is no longer there. And the dog hasn't learned anything constructive, such as being quiet in the crate.

If you don't give your dog a job that *you* approve of, he will become self-employed—and I promise you, you won't like his choice of employment.

Aggression can be easily (although not necessarily quickly) corrected by using positive methods. You can't answer aggression with aggression and expect the dog to become friendly. Doing that would be the same as if someone was yelling or hitting you because you were afraid.

CANINE CAVEATS

Two methods used in traditional training to show a dog "who's boss" are alpha rolls and scruff shakes. Grappling the dog to the ground and holding her in a submissive position is called an alpha roll. Grabbing the dog by the side of the neck, holding her off the ground, and yelling at her is called a scruff shake.

Please, pretty please, stay away from doing these! They will only frighten your dog and end up making her aggressive.

Myth #9: You Must Be Dominant Over Your Dog

There are still arguments going on in the dog training world about the word and intent of dominance. There are almost as many definitions of it as there are dog trainers. Yes there are dominant dogs, just as there are dominant people. I think the real problem is that in our society we tend to think of the word "dominant" as being punitive, violent, scheming, and coercive.

I feel the use of the word dominant clouds our perception of how to handle rules in training dogs. The goal is to accomplish compassionate leadership. Leadership between humans and dogs concerns boundaries and acceptable behaviors for dogs living with humans. Adding compassionate understanding in training clarifies the roles in our relationship. As a leader, the owner guides the dog, sets boundaries, and teaches what is acceptable, with compassion for the dog's perspective.

The behaviors humans cannot live with are usually natural canine behaviors, not attempts to subvert our leadership. Qualifying those behaviors as dominant is a misuse of the word and leads humans to believe there is intent from the dog where none exists.

I already mentioned in Chapter 1 that positive doesn't equal permissiveness, and that I never use physical or verbal punishment on my dogs. I don't rule by force and my dogs don't rule the roost. Being your dog's leader is really about showing them the ropes, teaching them the rules—with *compassion*—and being consistent with your cues.

I am sure you have all seen this scenario; you ask your dog to do something and he completely blows you off. And yet when your instructor takes the leash and a few treats, your dog acts like he has been trained for the Crufts Obedience Invitational. You get your dog back and he goes right back to ignoring you. Your dog isn't stubborn, stupid, or acting dominant. Your instructor probably has a clearer picture in her mind of what she wants the dog to do and your dog is reading that energy and complying.

Dominance has been attributed to many dog behaviors, most of which actually indicate an untrained dog, not a dominant one: licking, jumping up in greeting, pulling on the leash, getting up on the couch, a dog with separation anxiety that destroys the house in his terror of being left alone, peeing in the house, ripping up pillows, going out of doorways first, sitting on your foot, nudging your hand for petting, barking, biting the leash, or that you have to eat first before feeding your dog. I know of a woman that was told by her vet that when she came home from work and her dog started licking his legs (lick granuloma), that he was acting dominantly over her and she should alpha roll him. None of these behaviors are about your dog showing dominance over you; they are either indicative of an untrained dog or stress behaviors.

Myth #10: TV Shows Are Real Life

Lately there are a ton of shows on TV about dog training. Please just remember that television is all about *entertainment* (and ratings and money from advertisers). Just like the cop and lawyer and doctor shows, all have little to do with real life. You wouldn't go into a courtroom thinking you have learned all you need to know about the law from *Law and Order* or do surgery because you learned from *HOUSE.*

No one can train a dog or solve serious behavioral problems in 30 minutes. TV shows rarely have follow-up episodes to see how the so-called "cured" dogs are faring. An enormous amount of editing is involved, tons of information is left unsaid and unaddressed, and time lapses are not shown.

If your dog is having behavioral problems, please seek out a professional trainer, making sure to check references first.

Pop Quiz

1. If your dog is barking incessantly and you yell at the dog, what is your dog learning to do?

2. If your dog jumps on someone and you yank her down by the collar, what is your dog really learning?

3. If your dog is nervous and showing fear by either backing away or growling, what should you do?

The Least You Need to Know

- Positive training is based on proven scientific principles.
- Punishment training takes longer than positive training.
- Dogs always have choices in how they behave, regardless of the consequences and the training method.
- Positive training is the only reliable way to deal with aggression.

Side Effects of Punishment

In This Chapter

- Determining the causes of bad behavior and the effects of punishment
- Having *High Anxiety* and the *Fear Factor*
- Finding your dog ignoring you? Uh-oh …
- Keeping up your liability insurance: aggressive dogs
- Seeing beyond punishment: learned helplessness

Dogs are not humans. Maybe you're thinking, "Why are you telling me this? Of course I know my dog is not human!" Well, you may "know" it, but because you *are* human, you do "human" things and handle your dog in a "human" way. You can't help it. Therein lies the problem. How many people treat even inanimate objects as human? Yelling at the toaster, TV, and, of course, let's not forget our cars! Getting angry at these objects obviously doesn't make them work any better. Getting angry or punishing your dog will not make *him* better behaved, and can also create some serious side effects.

Punishment can create many toxic side effects. That doesn't mean I'm not sometimes tempted—I'm human after all, and at times my dogs annoy the heck out of me. But I never resort to it. Increased use of punishment does not stop "bad" behaviors. They just get worse.

The Negative Spiral of Punishment

Some dogs may tolerate more punishment than others. Some of them are happy, willing workers—or seem to be. After a while, however, they may shut down and refuse to work, or may develop neurotic behaviors that seemingly come out of nowhere.

What Is Punishment?

So what constitutes punishment to a dog? Anything can be: verbal reprimands, yelling, screaming, hitting, spanking, slapping, leash jerks, shock collars, head halters, choke collars, hoses, spray bottles, soda cans with pennies in them, citronella collars—anything that's meant to stop behaviors in a negative way.

A mommy dog may grab a puppy dog by the neck and reprimand the pup. What humans fail to see are the "okay, okay, I'll stop" signs that the puppy gives. Mommy dog sees these signs and relents immediately. Humans are simply incapable of detecting those signs because we are not dogs.

If you punish a dog and the dog says "uncle," you may have no clue and continue. The pup will now get really angry because she has been trying to say she's sorry, and yet you continue to pound her. She may then bite, growl, or become afraid of you. Perhaps she may feel the need to protect herself.

Now you have trained your puppy that, even if she submits, she is going to be punished anyway. This will lead to an aggressive, fearful dog, or one that goes into learned helplessness because she is not able to get the punishment to stop.

Escalating Punishment

Say your dog pulls on the leash. The first time, you yank him back. The next time, you yell at him. The third time, you hit him. Now you put a prong collar on him and continue to hit, yell, scream, and yank back. He is still pulling on the leash. And now, because of the punishment, he's possibly aggressing at people or dogs, and congratulations! *You* have now created a leash-aggressive dog!

Your dog jumps on people coming to the door. Today you push him down. He comes back for more. You push him down harder. Up he goes again. You knee him in the chest. He finally stops jumping. You are positively reinforced for using punishment because "it worked!" The next time he jumps, you will knee him in the chest.

Tomorrow he is jumping again. You start with kneeing him in the chest—because it worked yesterday. It isn't working today, so you squeeze his paws so tightly that he screams in pain. He stops jumping—today. *You* are reinforced again for using punishment: "Okay, *now* I get it—I have to squeeze his paws until he screams." And what will you do tomorrow?

Observable Effects of Punishment

You can't assume (because we all know what happens when we assume) that you know how an animal is feeling or what he's thinking, but you can observe and measure behaviors. Be careful when observing, though—some of these behaviors, especially avoidance, look to us imperfect humans as "guilt." They are not. Punish your dog and these six behaviors may happen in this order, and they can be reliably observed and measured:

- **Anxiety:** Marked by "shut-down" behaviors
- **Fear:** Marked by "get away" behaviors
- **Escape:** Observable behavior
- **Avoidance:** Observable behavior
- **Aggression:** Observable behavior
- **Learned helplessness:** Observable behavior

Many people will then punish their dog for displaying these behaviors, which only escalates the dog's response.

Causes of "Bad" Behaviors

There are many causes of "bad" behaviors, most of which can be alleviated. The top three sources of these reactions are the following:

- Punishment from humans
- Punishment from other animals
- Punishment from the environment

Additional stimuli that can create different levels of arousal include thunder, grooming, vet visits, people, other dogs, other animals, cars, bikes, kids, being left alone, large groups, buildings, petting, toenail clipping, being on leash, men, hats, umbrellas, grass, concrete, gravel, linoleum, balloons, fireworks—you name it, there's a dog out there afraid of it.

What is the root of these problems? It can be many things, including improper socialization, or none at all. An owner may mistakenly manage the dog's environment too much in the critical early stages to such a degree that the dog is never exposed to loud noises, pots dropping, new sights, and so on. When the dog gets older and these daily things occur, the dog freaks out. You certainly don't want to *over*expose your young dog, but in real life, stuff happens. A fearful mother dog can pass along her neurosis. And the *biggie* is punishment from us for reacting out of nervousness or fear.

You may do one of two things when your dog shows signs of fear:

- Try to soothe and pet the dog: "It's okay Rover, Uncle Bob won't bite you."
- Yell and smack the dog: "Don't you *dare* growl at Aunt Helen!"

Either way, your response is reinforcing the dog for the behavior you don't want. If you try to comfort the dog, the dog is reinforced for the fearful or aggressive behaviors. If you punish the dog, still thinking that you have to show the dog when she's wrong (although how a dog can be "wrong" for being afraid is beyond me), you're creating the wrong association—she then learns that bad things happen around that stimulus, and be even more afraid! Because the dog is already in stress mode, where she's unable to think at all, you have just added even more stress and pain. The next time she encounters that particular stimulus, her negative reaction will intensify and escalate faster.

Very often our reactions or punishment create worse problems than we started with. What may have started out as mild anxiety can quickly grow into full-blown aggression.

> **POOCH POINTERS**
>
> It's not up to us to decide for our dogs, or anyone else for that matter, what's scary or not scary. What we humans may perceive as benign may be perceived by each individual dog as horrible. I love thunderstorms, yet one of my friends is so afraid of them, she hides in the closet and cries.
>
> Before I found a wonderful computer technician, if I was having problems with a program, I would yell, scream, rant, and rave, and all but smash my computer with a sledge hammer. My dogs would then freak out at my behavior and display all sorts of appeasement behaviors at me (such as jumping, pawing at me, licking, frantic tail wagging, hiding under the table, etc.), thinking I was screaming at them. This, of course, would make me even angrier! I learned that if I am about to beat my computer to death, I should put the dogs out in the yard.

Lions and Tigers and Bears, Oh My! Anxiety and Fear

What's happening after you punish the dog either verbally or physically? He becomes anxious and tries to appease and diffuse your anger with submissive doggie gestures. Some of the signs of a dog's anxiety that we humans incorrectly perceive as "looking guilty" may be a lowered head, tail tucked between legs, ears back, and even a submissive grin. We assume (there's that word again) that the dog "knows what he did wrong."

The observable signs of anxiety can also include the following:

- Nervousness
- Pacing
- Whining
- Drooling
- Sniffing
- Yawning
- Barking
- Chewing
- Obsessive licking (licking feet or body parts compulsively enough to cause sores—also called lick granuloma)
- Inattention to owner and many of the signals listed in Chapter 5

Think about it from your own perspective: you have a boss who's very punishing—nothing you ever do is right. You go to work each day with a heavy heart and dragging feet. You start to develop physical or emotional symptoms related to anxiety disorders. You may still be able to function, but you'll do the absolute minimum, cut corners, and shirk responsibility whenever possible.

To think that your dog will suffer no side effects when you punish him is downright unreasonable. If there were no effects of punishment, then "anxiety disorder" wouldn't be in the dictionary!

Fear is another consequence of using punishment. Some of the signs of fear can be the following:

- Hiding
- Hackles up
- Wide eyes
- Growling
- Backing away

- Evacuation of bowels

- Shaking

You're out walking your dog and it starts raining. She sees an umbrella for the first time and is terrified. She starts to shake, her hackles go up, and she tries vehemently to get away from this horribly scary thing. You're embarrassed by her behavior in such a public place and you chastise her. The next time you innocently pop open the umbrella, she may very well start to growl, shake, or evacuate her bowels. I'm sure you've observed these types of behaviors at the vet's office.

Your dog soils the house in your absence. You come home and yell at her. Of course, she has no clue why you're punishing her. So she learns that "homecoming" is a stressful and fearful time.

Maybe you're from the school of thought that advocates "don't punish unless you catch her in the act." If so, you then lay in wait for her to soil the house and then whammo! You punish the dog. What has the dog learned then? To be afraid of you and to run and hide and soil behind the couch where you can't see her because eliminating around you is dangerous.

 DOGGIE DATA

A woman called me to ask about housetraining. It turns out her dog runs away from her when she tries to approach. When I asked her what she was doing, she said she was hitting the dog for soiling the house. I explained that punishment is not the proper or effective way to housetrain a dog. Her response was, "Oh, I don't punish my dog; I only hit her."

I'm Not Deaf, I'm Ignoring You: Escape and Avoidance

Next up on the countdown of behaviors caused by punishment are escape and avoidance. They're actually quite similar—it all depends on how the dog manifests them.

Escape can include the following:

- Running away

- Digging out of the yard or kennel

- Scratching at doors

- Hiding under or behind furniture

- Slipping out of collars

If your dog would rather be lost in the woods, eat bark from trees, sleep out in the raw elements without any of the creature comforts such as air-conditioning, heat, running water, three square meals per day, and a soft bed, then you may want to reexamine your relationship with your dog.

If, at the slightest opportunity, your dog flies out of the door ("I'm outta here!"), what do you think may be the problem? The correct answer is *not*: "My dog is a (*fill in the breed here*), so of course he runs away." Breed has nothing to do with a dog running away—chances are you're using punishment to train your dog and he wants to get away from it.

Avoidance is the other half of this equation. There are two kinds of avoidance: passive avoidance and active avoidance. Passive avoidance includes the following:

- Ignoring

- Avoiding eye contact or petting

- "Selective deafness"

Active avoidance includes the following:

- Not coming when called

- Staying out of reach

- Inattention to owner

CANINE CAVEATS

I mean it. If your dog is displaying the early warning signs of anxiety, fear, escape, and avoidance, *do not* wait any longer to fix these using positive methods. If you increase your punishment to try to correct the problem, be sure your insurance is paid up, because this dog will become a danger to you and others.

Avoidance, whether it's active or passive, is probably one of the most widely used reactions to punishment. Dogs do it, humans do it, and maybe even the birds and bees do it. For those of us who hate confrontation, avoidance is the way to go. Dogs have all sorts of rituals linked to avoiding conflict. The calming signals that dogs send to each other are all about avoiding aggression and "arguments." If you see your dog "blowing you off," look at yourself and see if you're stressing him. I promise you, he is not being dominant or disobedient—he is most likely stressed in some way by your behavior.

As the punishment in their lives increases, escape and avoidance behaviors are the last maneuvers dogs use before aggression starts. This is the last level you can attain using punishment before your problems really shoot through the roof. Start positive training *now* to regain your dog's trust.

Meltdown: Aggression

Aggression can be a learned behavior. That's hard to comprehend sometimes, and you may try to justify and explain away the aggression by saying, "Well, what do you expect from a (*insert name of breed here*)?" That only gets rid of any guilt or denial you may feel; it doesn't help you get out of the problem that punishment caused.

The breed of dog may have nothing to do with aggression. Yes, some breeds are specifically bred to do certain jobs requiring force, but bad training methods are bad training methods. Period. Answer aggression with aggression, and think you'll get a happy, well-adjusted dog? Think again! I've worked with many of the so-called "aggressive" breeds and found them to be wonderfully smart, sweet, and teachable.

Signs of Aggression

Some of the more obvious signs of aggression are the following:

- Growling
- Biting
- Snarling
- Snapping
- Attacking

When I come across a dog who growls at me, I get down and kiss her feet (well, not literally) and thank her for warning me. Punish the dog for giving off a warning and guess what? You won't get warnings anymore—you'll just get a bite.

Types and Causes of Aggression

There are many, many causes of aggression, and many of them can be corrected. Some people who own aggressive dogs may even deliberately encourage the dog because they enjoy the feeling of power or of feeling protected.

Here is a short list of causes:

- Territoriality
- Feeling vulnerable to attack by other dogs (such as forcing their heads away by the use of head halters)
- Influx of new members to the household (canine or human)
- Resource guarding: can be food, objects, or humans
- Seasonal hormonal fluctuations, such as breeding, arousal level, or cycling females
- Physical stress: injury, illness, drugs, reactions to collars or corrections
- Responses to punishment

- *Scheduled induced aggression:* incorrect use of a reinforcement schedule

- Our responses to aggression: accidental reinforcement

- Observational learning: allowing dogs to chase or attack other animals

MUTTLEY MEANINGS

Scheduled induced aggression is aggressive behavior that occurs when the results you get don't match your expectations. You know that if you put money in a soda machine, your purchase comes out. If you put money in and nothing comes out, what do you do? You may kick the machine, pound on it, rock it, or grab a sledgehammer and smash it. Why? Because you've *learned* that putting money into the machine is supposed to get you a soda. When it doesn't, you get angry!

Correcting Aggression

The first step in controlling and preventing aggression is understanding the situations that frequently trigger the aggressive responses in your dog. After you're aware, avoid putting him in those situations as much as possible, to reduce the need (from the dog's perspective) to exhibit that behavior.

Although punishment (from humans) may initially *suppress* aggressive behaviors, dogs learn to mask the early observable (to humans) aggressive signals to avoid punishment. Punishment can actually lead to and cause a variety of negative manifestations, including aggression.

Remember when I said aggression can be a learned behavior? Aggression, from the dog's point of view, keeps the animal safe from danger. If a scary thing appears out of nowhere and startles the dog, the dog aggresses, and the scary thing either goes away or the owner takes the dog away. The aggressive behavior worked and will be repeated the next time the dog is afraid.

> **DOGGIE DATA**
>
> Buddy lived in a household with three other dogs. When a fifth dog was brought in, Buddy did an about-face in behavior. Even though he used to be a "doggie diplomat"—very gentle and nice to strange dogs—he became fearful and would growl and snap at other dogs.
>
> What happened? It turns out that the fifth dog was very punishing to Buddy, and Buddy was showing redirected aggression to other dogs. When the fifth dog was managed better and the punishing stopped, Buddy went back to being his normal, sweet self.
>
> And was the fifth dog punished? No way! He was heavily reinforced for presenting friendly behavior, and soon stopped bullying Buddy on his own!

Learned Helplessness

If you increase your punishment so much so that the dog no longer has any other recourse or alternatives to protect himself, you'll create learned helplessness. Think of it as doggie depression. Some of the signs are the following:

- Cowering
- Rolling over
- Submission
- Eyes glazed over
- Motionless (can be frozen in a submissive posture)
- Appearing catatonic or deaf

Behavioral science shows us that continual use of inescapable punishment teaches the dog to do literally nothing: to be helpless. As the punishment escalates, the level of intensity of the dog's reactions will increase from anxiety right up to learned helplessness. If the intensity of the punishment is so high with no escape possible, *all* mammals will go into learned helplessness.

Efforts to prod him into action will most likely be ineffectual. Even when presented with further punishment, the dog will do nothing further to avoid the punishment, and will just endure quietly whatever additional castigation you dole out.

I hope I have convinced you to cease and desist any and all punishments. I don't care what behavior problem you have; punishment is *never* warranted.

Pop Quiz

1. What does your dog find punishing?

2. What are the six observable effects of punishment?

3. Have you noticed lately any of the signs of anxiety in your dog?

The Least You Need to Know

- Causes of bad behaviors can include punishment from humans, other dogs, and the environment.
- If you aren't ignoring bad behavior, you *are* reinforcing it.
- Punishment only makes us feel better; it does nothing to stop bad behaviors.
- Punishment creates more problems, such as anxiety, fear, escape, avoidance, aggression, and learned helplessness.

How Dogs Learn and Communicate

Continuing on our incredible journey, here's where you find out how dogs learn, how to positively fix mistakes and even stop them from happening in the first place, and how to understand what your dog is telling you. Dogs do have a language all their own (and it isn't English). We can learn to read them and speak to them, and use our knowledge to train them and keep them safe and happy. This part will also get you started on eye contact and focus, name response, come, and teaching your dog to accept handling.

After reading Part 1, you might see some mistakes that you've already made with your dog. Not to worry. Dogs are amazingly adaptable and resilient, so you can fix these problems with positive methods.

Learning Their ABCs

In This Chapter

- The ABCs of learning
- Math revisited: negative, positive, reinforcement, punishment
- Good and bad associations
- Classical and operant conditioning are always happening

As I touched on a little in Chapter 1, the basis of all learning (for both humans and dogs) happens within either classical conditioning or operant conditioning.

Learning is a change in behavior due to experience. As a teacher to your dog, you want to make as many of their experiences pleasant as possible. Behavior is influenced by its consequences. You reward or punish people and dogs so that they will behave in different ways.

The Basis of All Learning

There are three components to every *learned* behavior. Just remember your ABCs:

- **Antecedent:** A cue, or something that comes before a behavior
- **Behavior:** What the animal does, resulting from the cue
- **Consequence:** What happens directly after the behavior

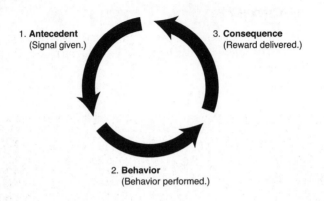

The sequence in which operant conditioning happens. You can't have the behavior before the antecedent, and you can't have the consequence before the behavior.

A Is for Antecedent

An antecedent, more commonly called a "cue," is anything that happens *before* a behavior. You're surrounded daily by all kinds of antecedents, and you adjust your behavior accordingly. This can be a red traffic light, a lightning bolt, the alarm clock, the promise of a paycheck, the doorbell ringing, or Mom saying "Let's all go for ice cream!" To a dog, antecedents can include a person approaching, the can opener, or seeing the leash coming out. These are all antecedents that tell a person or dog how to react next.

B Is for Behavior

"B" is for behavior—or how you or your dog respond to the antecedent. The red light tells you to stop, the lightning bolt tells you to run for cover, the alarm clock wakes you up, the promise of a paycheck inspires you to work, a doorbell ringing means answer the door, and "ice cream" is … well, that's pretty obvious. To a dog, a person approaching means jump up and display submissive behavior, like licking and pawing at the person (unless you've trained him that a person approaching is a cue to sit). Hearing the can opener means run to the kitchen, and seeing the leash coming out of the closet means run to the door.

A dog that has been taught to understand that a person approaching is a cue to sit.
(Photo by P. Dennison)

C Is for Consequence

So what happens when you've seen the antecedent and done the behavior? Now comes the "C," the consequence. Stop at a red light and you won't get into an accident or get a ticket. Run for cover and you won't get struck by lightning. Wake up when the alarm rings and you won't be late for work. Pick up your paycheck and you get to go shopping and pay your bills. Answer the doorbell, Publishers Clearing House is there, and you've won a million dollars! (Now you don't have to set the alarm to get up and go to work!) Again, the ice cream is obvious.

The dog gets attention for jumping (or for sitting), she gets fed after the can is opened, and she goes for a walk after the leash is put on.

The behavior and consequence can also be something good or bad and can change. For instance, if you allow your puppy to bite you when you're playing with him, here's how you've trained your dog:

- You get down on the floor (antecedent).
- The dog bites you for attention (behavior).
- You play with the dog to get him to stop biting you (consequence).

Now the dog is older and you no longer want him to bite you, so here's what you can do:

- You get down on the floor (antecedent).
- The dog bites you with adult teeth and it hurts (behavior).
- You punish the dog by hitting or yelling at him, or you use the proper positive trainer response, which is to get up and leave (consequence).

CANINE CAVEATS

Please don't allow a puppy to do what you won't want her to do as an adult dog. It will only confuse and stress the dog, and annoy the heck out of you.

The Main Principles of Operant Conditioning

Positive reinforcement, negative reinforcement, positive punishment, and negative punishment are the main terms of operant conditioning, and these can be confusing at first.

In science, the terms "positive" and "negative" relate only to adding something or taking something away. The terms "reinforcement" and "punishment" relate to behavior increasing or decreasing:

- **Positive Reinforcement (+R):** Anything that is *added* (positive) that *increases* (reinforces) behavior.

- **Positive Punishment (+P):** Anything that is *added* (positive) that *decreases* (punishes) behavior.

- **Negative Reinforcement (–R):** Anything that is *taken away* (negative) to *increase* (reinforce) behavior.

- **Negative Punishment (–P):** Anything that is *taken away* (negative) to *decrease* (punishes) behavior.

Now that you're thoroughly confused, the following sections give you some examples to help you gain a better understanding of these concepts.

Positive Reinforcement

Here are some examples: your dog sits when you ask her to and you give her a treat; her sitting behavior will increase in the future. Give your dog treats for walking on a loose leash, and her loose-leash-walking behavior will increase. Reinforce your dog for not rearranging the furniture, and "lying down calmly" behaviors will increase. Reinforce your dog for having "four on the floor," and her staying-on-the-floor behavior will increase.

POOCH POINTERS

Positive reinforcement establishes "good" behaviors faster, creating a love of learning and a great relationship. Positive reinforcement doesn't create confusion and stress or any bad behaviors—unless you reinforce "bad" behaviors.

Positive Punishment

Don't be confused by this—positive means something added, and it isn't necessarily something nice. Your dog is barking and you turn on the citronella collar. His barking may decrease. Your dog urinates on the rug and you hit him with a newspaper. His eliminating on the rug behavior may decrease. You touch a hot stove and burn your hand. You will not touch a hot stove again.

Please don't get the wrong idea here—I am *not* advocating positive punishment. In fact, I highly recommend that you stay away from it. There are too many toxic side effects. The timing has to be perfect (if you punish the dog for soiling the house after she comes to you, you have just punished her for coming to you), and punishment is associated with the person giving it.

Positive punishment often only suppresses behavior: sure, the dog stops urinating on the carpet, but now he does it behind the couch. For some dogs, barking is so self-reinforcing (they like to bark) that they'll bark regardless of what you do, or bark only when the shock or citronella collar is off. The punishment has to outweigh the rewards and the motivation for it to be effective.

Depending on the motivation, some people (and dogs) will go to great lengths to succeed over adversity, continuing to practice their success-seeking behaviors regardless of punishment or hardships.

 CANINE CAVEATS

You really can't get rid of Pavlov. You positively punish your dog by shocking him with an electric shock collar when he barks in his crate to get him to stop the barking. He now has the association that being in his crate is a horrible thing.

Negative Reinforcement

Negative reinforcement increases a behavior by taking something away that the dog doesn't like. Of course, you must have already added these punishers to be able to then take them away.

So what starts out as positive punishment can end up being negative reinforcement. The choke collar is yanked and then loosened up when the dog stops pulling. You hit the dog and then stop hitting him when he ceases to jump. The electricity is turned off, and then turned back on after you pay the bill.

As with positive punishment—don't do it!

Negative Punishment

This sounds like the most awful option, doesn't it? It isn't, though, and in fact is the method of choice that positive trainers use to punish their dogs. I did tell you that I do punish my dogs and this is how I do it.

We humans are controlled primarily through negative reinforcement. We're punished when we haven't done what is reinforcing to those who are in charge (be it parents, employers, or trainers). Positive reinforcement has, unfortunately, been used less often, but it is more effective than negative reinforcement and has fewer unwanted side effects.

For example, a student is punished when he doesn't study. He may study after that, but he may also stay away from school (truancy), vandalize school property, attack teachers, or do nothing. With positive reinforcement, the student would have been reinforced for studying in the first place, and most likely would have learned to love learning.

Negative punishment reduces behaviors by taking away or withholding something good or something the dog will work for. Your dog jumps on you and you walk away, thus withholding the attention she craves. Her jumping behavior will decrease.

Your dog is being pushy and demanding attention. You walk away, denying the dog your attention. The next time your dog will sit politely for attention, reducing the pushy behavior. You ask your dog to sit and she looks at you blankly. You withhold the treat. The next time you ask her to sit, she will sit, reducing the "looking at you blankly" behavior.

You're playing ball with your dog and she brings it back but won't drop it. You end the game. The next time you play ball, she will drop the ball, reducing the "hold on to the ball at all costs" behavior. The bad do bad because the bad is rewarded. The good do good because the good is rewarded.

Ring a Bell? Classical Conditioning

Classical conditioning is an association between two *stimuli*. One is neutral and in the beginning has no meaning. The other stimulus is one that already has meaning for the dog (or human). The stimulus can be pleasant, or it can be unpleasant.

MUTTLEY MEANINGS

Stimuli (the plural of stimulus) are any events that affect or are capable of affecting behavior.

The two main events that humans or dogs don't need to learn to react to are food and pain. Almost everything else is a learned association.

Let's go back (just for a minute) to Pavlov and the metronome and the dog and the saliva. When Pavlov first started pairing the sound of the metronome just before food was presented, the dogs did not drool. However, over time, with consistent pairing (metronome and then food), the dogs began to salivate at the sound of the metronome. As far as their automatic reactions were concerned, the metronome meant food.

Why Is Classical Conditioning Used?

Classical conditioning is used for two reasons:

- To create an association between a stimulus that would not normally have any meaning along with a stimulus that would have meaning

- To train automatic responses (drooling, blinking, even emotions)

Of course, you don't really need to teach your dog to blink or drool, but the emotion part is important. The recess bell has no meaning until it's paired with playtime; "Sit" has no meaning unless paired with sitting; and the smoke alarm has no meaning until you smell smoke.

> **CANINE CAVEATS**
>
> Why is the *order* in which things are associated important? Because if you say "Sit" while the dog is standing and continue to say "Sit," then the dog will learn that "Sit" means to stand. If you want your dog to sit when you say "Sit," then pair the word *with the action of sitting.*

Classical conditioning is largely responsible for the *reflexive* motivation to respond in any situation. For example, if you smell bread baking, you feel hungry and possibly even start salivating.

Operant behavior is *voluntary* behavior that is influenced by its consequences. You smell bread baking and get out a plate and some butter. Whether wanted behaviors occur in the future depends on the nature of the consequence. If doing the behavior makes life better for the dog (or for you, for that matter), it will most likely keep happening.

Your dog meets a person who gives him lots of yummy treats. The next time he meets that person, he'll be happy to see her (and will probably salivate)! Associations, especially first ones, are vitally important to how a dog views his world. You can easily create a happy, well-adjusted dog or a fearful, aggressive dog by the associations you allow him to have.

Bad Associations

Setting up a dog to be fearful or aggressive is easy to do: just make sure all her associations are bad ones. For example, let your dog meet someone who will knee her in the chest or yell if she jumps. The next time she meets that person, your dog won't be happy to see him or her. Do this enough times and your dog will be fearful of people.

Here are some other ways to set up bad associations: introduce your young puppy to an older dog who isn't good around puppies, and watch your puppy grow fearful or aggressive toward strange dogs. Yell at your dog for myriad "bad" behaviors and she'll learn to either ignore you or be afraid of you. Call your dog to come and then punish her for something she did an hour ago, and the word "Come" will now take on a negative connotation. Hit your dog for growling at a child and watch your dog learn to hate children (and probably progress from growling to biting). Punish your dog for making a mistake during training and she will then associate training with pain, which certainly does nothing to help her love learning.

CANINE CAVEATS

Beware of "negative" associative learning. Your dog runs away and comes back an hour later. You punish him for running away—only he understands it as punishment for returning. The next time you say "Come," he will stay away because that word was paired with unpleasant results.

Keeping Those Good Associations Happenin'

So what *can* you do? Make sure the associations are good ones! Have your puppy play with friendly dogs and meet nice, dog-friendly people. Use positive reinforcement as your training philosophy. Get rid of punishments from people, dogs, and (as much as possible) the environment.

Whenever you run across something potentially scary that you want your dog not to be neurotic about, just add some positive stimuli and it will turn out all right. Let's say your dog is afraid of other dogs barking. The next time you hear a dog barking, offer your dog lots of treats, before he becomes afraid. If your dog is afraid of people approaching, pair food with a person approaching.

Use associations properly and just be cognizant that Pavlov is always sitting on your shoulder—24 hours a day, 7 days a week. Always be happy and nice, like Ronald McDonald, Bozo the Clown, and Howdy Doody all rolled up in one. It's a jungle out there—don't become one of the "bad guys."

> **POOCH POINTERS**
>
> Yes, even the environment can be punishing. Inanimate objects can be dangerous! Lamps can fall, baby gates can get stuck on doggies' necks, doors can slam in faces, and paws can get stuck in crate doors. Honking horns and wailing sirens can send many a dog under the table in fear.

Pop Quiz

1. Define antecedent, behavior, and cue.

2. Can you come up with your own examples of positive reinforcement, positive punishment, negative reinforcement, and negative punishment?

The Least You Need to Know

- All learned behaviors have an antecedent, a behavior, and a consequence.
- Positive reinforcement creates the most reliable behaviors.
- Negative punishment is the best way to punish your dog.
- Make sure all of your dog's associations are pleasant ones.

What Is Your Dog Telling You?

In This Chapter

- Recognizing the canine peacekeeping system
- Learning how to stop stressing out your dog!
- Discovering dog talk and how to recognize it
- Using your knowledge of canine body language to your benefit

Dogs are pack animals, and it's important for animals who live in a pack (wolves, dogs, humans) to have ritualized methods for avoiding aggression and conflict. Every species on this planet owns its own set of rules and regulations. Dogs give out 48 signals that we as humans can perceive. We give 12 signals to dogs that the dogs perceive as aggressive or threatening.

This chapter shows you the signals your dog is trying to give you, and also tells you what signals you might be sending back without realizing it. Then you'll learn some ways to communicate using the dog's own language.

Turid Rugaas, a Norwegian dog trainer, has coined the words "calming signals" to describe how dogs communicate. Please see the reading list in Appendix B.

Why Dogs Give Off Calming Signals

We all possess certain signs or *precursors* that signify "I won't hurt you; I am a nice wolf/dog/person." Although dogs do show some threatening signals—growling, barking, lunging, teeth baring—they show even more signals to avoid conflict. We must learn to inhibit our aggression—otherwise the pack will not survive. If there were no stopgaps, we'd all just kill each other and die out as a species.

 MUTTLEY MEANINGS

A **precursor** is a sign that something is going to happen. This can be a signal that the dog is getting nervous or happy or afraid.

In this country, making direct eye contact and reaching out to shake hands are seen as proper greeting behaviors. If someone refused to look at you or shake your hand, you'd feel uncomfortable or possibly suspicious. In other countries, direct eye contact and shaking hands might be perceived as a threat or the height of bad manners.

Just as people from different cultures don't always understand each other's signals, people have trouble interpreting the signals that dogs give out. Dogs do in fact have a language, and I promise you, it isn't English.

Understanding Your Dog's Precursor Signs

Get rid of any notion that your dog feels guilt, shame, and the like. Why? Because dogs are dogs! These are human emotions and dogs are a different species. However, dogs do have a very strict system of manners with fitting responses.

We humans are, for the most part, clueless regarding these behavioral responses because we're not dogs. We have this persistent misconception—and apparently it's difficult to let go of—that dogs are really people in disguise. An inability to communicate effectively with dogs is the overwhelming cause for almost every canine "behavior" problem. It's really a human problem, not a dog problem.

In doggie land, communication is accomplished through a series of complex sounds, facial and body movements, and scents. The combination changes all the time and the meanings are different each time. If the first sequence of signs is ignored, they will increase in intensity, and additional behaviors will appear. Say a child or adult is doing something that the dog regards as threatening. The dog may signal, nonverbally at first, that he's not happy with your behavior. The adult or child doesn't notice and continues to pressure the dog. (Don't worry—we'll outline the signals coming up.)

DOGGIE DATA

Marshall brought his seven-year-old Boxer, Brandy, to see me. Brandy had been biting Marshall's one-year-old son in the face. Marshall loved his dog and was determined to fix this problem. After Marshall learned the dog's signals, he was able to move his son away from the dog before the signals escalated. Within three weeks, the dog had completely stopped bothering the little boy.

The dog may use additional nonverbal signals and is ignored again. And again. The dog's signals may now include some verbal noises, such as a low growl. If the warnings are continually ignored, and the dog has been unable to make his point politely (within his own frame of reference), the dog's signals will escalate into lifting his lip, snarling, showing teeth, and snapping or biting.

DOGGIE DATA

Lisa was volunteering in a shelter for homeless dogs. Shelters are very stressful places, and she wanted to help reduce their stress. After learning to recognize these signals, she utilized them during her visits. Within a few days, the dogs in the kennels were barking less, calming down faster, and able to focus better during the retraining process.

These types of behaviors didn't come out of nowhere—you just weren't paying attention.

Is Your Dog Stressed?

Life is stressful. Some stress is good and some can be devastating, both mentally and physically. Teaching your dog to accept a certain amount of anxiety is vital in creating a happy and healthy dog who will bounce back quickly from everyday stress. Here are the more common causes of stress. Some of them you can forestall and prevent; some you can't.

Stressed-Out Puppies

Here are some possible causes of stress for puppies:

- Stressed mother
- Born into a puppy mill—including being taken away from mom and siblings too soon, the truck ride, and the pet shop
- Environment change (even when you get the dog from a reputable breeder)
- Isolation or lack of proper food, water, or social contact (dogs are pack animals)
- Tail docking, ear cropping, dewclaw removal
- Travel
- Improper socialization, or none at all

Stress for Adult Dogs

Here are some causes of stress for adult dogs:

- Moving, being given up for adoption, dumped, or abandoned
- Suddenly taking the dog to new places without training her to accept distractions with positive results in a variety of situations
- Competitive dog sports, such as agility (see Chapter 18)
- Not having been socialized as a puppy

- Sickness

- Too little or too much exercise

- Punishment

- Grooming

- Dissension in pack (human or canine)

- Being punished every time he gives the owner precursor signs that he is nervous ("please don't be angry with me"), which makes him confused and frustrated

- Inconsistency in training

- Bitches coming into heat—stressful for both the bitch and any males who are around

What the 48 Dog Signals Are

The following are 48 perceptible calming signals that dogs give off:

- Head turning away

Head turn, lip licking, and paw raised in avoidance.
(Photo by P. Dennison)

- Howling
- Eyes turning away
- Growling
- Yawning
- Spinning/circling
- Panting, heavy breathing
- Stopped or frozen (in an awkward position)
- Drooling
- Sniffing

Sniffing when play becomes too rough.
(Photo by P. Dennison)

- Lip licking
- Short attention span
- Raising a paw (as if to "shake")
- Biting the leash
- Whining
- Poop eating
- Barking
- Grass eating
- Water drinking
- Marking
- Pooping
- Aggressing
- Avoiding

Head down and moving away in avoidance.
(Photo by P. Dennison)

Two dogs studiously avoiding each other.
(Photo by P. Dennison)

- Hyper behavior
- Slow, reluctant behaviors
- Complete body turns away from you
- Play bows
- *Arcing* (or curving)

MUTTLEY MEANINGS

When dogs approach each other and wish to avoid fights, they **arc** around each other rather than approach head on. They will arc in a big circle, at times even curving their bodies. This can calm the other dog and avoid a potential conflict.

- Sitting
- Lying down

- Frantically wagging tail
- Shaking (as if they were shaking off water)
- *Hackles* raised
- *Splitting*

MUTTLEY MEANINGS

When one dog runs between two other dogs who are playing rough, he's **splitting.** He splits from the rear for obvious reasons (there are no teeth in the rear). Dogs often split up humans, too. This isn't jealousy; it's the dog's perception that the closeness is dangerous. **Hackles** are the hair along the spine or neck. The dog's hackles rise up when he is nervous.

Two dogs meet and one dog arcs (curves) her body.
(Photo by P. Dennison)

Enticing another dog to play by offering a submissive down.
(Photo by P. Dennison)

Rolling over in submission: "Don't eat me!"
(Photo by P. Dennison)

Splitting up too-rough play.
(Photo by P. Dennison)

- Blinking the eyes
- Body shaking (as if he is cold)
- Sneezing
- Scratching
- Sweaty paws
- Raised pulse rate
- Raised temperature (ears can get hot)
- "Stress" shedding and dandruff
- Chewing
- Digging
- Diarrhea
- Loss of appetite (won't take treats)

The Border Collie is lifting his lip. The Schnauzer is very stiff.
(Photo by P. Dennison)

- Head lowered
- Showing teeth

Ambiguous Signals

Many of the calming signals just listed are natural, normal behaviors, so you have to look at the context in which the dog is doing those things. If the dog has just finished playing or if it's a hot day, drinking would be a normal behavior. If, however, there is another dog around who is pestering your dog, water drinking would be a sign that she's nervous.

Grass eating is usually a sign of one of three things:

- The dog has an upset tummy and she needs to throw up (and will most likely do so on your bed).
- The dog is missing some nutrients from her diet.
- The dog is stressed.

Dogs will often "graze" when meeting someone new (be it a person or another dog).

A play bow can be an invitation to play, or it can be a sign of nervousness. I always look at the other dog to see what the play bow really means. If the other dog then plays, the bow was intended to entice. If the other dog goes off sniffing or engaging in other behaviors, the bow was presented as an "I am nervous" signal.

One dog enticing another dog to play utilizing a play bow.
(Photo by P. Dennison)

Yawning and lip licking can also have two meanings. They can be natural—the dog is tired and yawns, or he's drawing in scent by licking. Or they can be signs of stress.

Personal Stress Signals

In addition, there are also what I call "personal" stress signals. These are different for every dog and can involve any of the following:

- The set of his ears and tail

- Any creases on his face

- The shape of his nose and muzzle, which often changes when a dog feels stressed

- The look and shape of his eyes and pupils

- Foaming at the mouth (different than drooling)

- Tightness of his mouth when taking food

- Suppleness or tightness of his body and face

- Puffing out of cheeks with short but explosive breaths

CANINE CAVEATS

It's extremely important for you to learn to read your own dog's personal signals so that you can avert potential problems.

Every dog is a little different. Some dogs have cropped ears or tails and so some of these signals don't apply. Some dogs show their nervousness by enlargement of their pupils, but in some dogs it's the complete opposite—their pupils get very tiny.

Yawning.
(Photo by P. Dennison)

12 Human Signals

Humans don't even think about most of these signals when approaching a dog—any dog, be it your own or a strange dog. Others are tenets of negative training philosophies. I hope you will think about them now, because you might be stressing your dog out continually, which is an accident waiting to happen.

Here are the stressful signals you might be giving your dog:

- Leaning over the dog
- Forcing your face in the dog's face
- Petting the dog on the withers (shoulder blade) area
- Petting the dog around the face and especially on the top of the head
- Walking straight into the dog
- Eye contact (with a strange dog)
- Hands reaching down to the dog

Here are five of the threatening postures that relate to punishment-based training methods. You won't do these anymore, will you?

- "Alpha" rolls
- Scruff shakes
- Hitting
- Yelling
- Forcing the dog into position (such as a "sit" or "down")

Can you teach your dogs to accept the first seven human signals without becoming fearful or aggressive? Of course you can, and you must. It is imperative to teach your dog to accept all types of obnoxious human behavior. If you don't, you're headed for some big problems.

CANINE CAVEATS

Some people may tell you that you have to be dominant over your dog, show 'em who's boss, or that you should "be the alpha." They're assuming that you need to punish your dog to be in control. This will only get you into trouble by creating other far-reaching problems—aggression, avoidance, or shy behaviors.

Humans can't replicate a true canine alpha. By incorrectly viewing aggressive behaviors as the proper way to rule dogs, you can't expect the dogs to be happy and willing participants in your relationship. Be your dog's benevolent leader, not a malevolent dictator. Rule with kindness and consistency. Be clear about what you want and you'll never need to dominate your dog into submission.

Person leaning over a dog in an inappropriate way.
(Photo by P. Dennison)

Ways to Reduce Your Dog's Stress

Except for the more disgusting things such as marking, poop eating, grass eating, and the like, humans can communicate directly to dogs using the same language they use. You can very effectively use the following in most cases:

- Avert your eyes
- Avert your face
- Turn your back on the dog
- Walk slowly away
- Freeze in position
- Yawn
- Lick your lips
- Sit
- Lie down
- Kneel on the ground and pluck grass
- Turn sideways
- Blink
- Split
- Arc or curve
- Walk parallel to the dog

Instead of forcing yourself on a dog, use these signs to entice him to come to you. A typical greeting can be the following:

- Glance in the dog's direction and quickly avert your eyes, or even blink a few times.
- While looking away, lick your lips and/or yawn.
- Glance back again; then turn your head and body away from the dog.

- Move away slowly for a few steps.

- Squat or kneel down, turning your body sideways to the dog.

- Keep your hands to yourself. Let your arms drop naturally by your side and wait for the dog to approach.

If at any time the dog sniffs the ground, avoids you, yawns, or licks his lips, you may answer him back with some of your own signals. Be sure to discontinue the approach and just move away slowly. Never pressure a dog to say "hello." That's just setting the dog up to be more nervous or fearful.

By learning these signals, becoming fluent in "dog," and practicing them yourself, you can effectively learn to communicate with most dogs and avert potential disasters.

Homework

Read over this chapter a few times and pick a few signals, such as lip licking, turning the head away, and yawning. Then watch your dog(s) carefully for a week and become "fluent" in those signals. Next week, pick a few more signals, continue to observe your dog, and memorize those signals. Continue in this vein until you can really see the small subtleties of your dog's behavior.

You will find that a whole new fascinating world has opened up for you, and you'll have a greater understanding and appreciation for your dog.

The Least You Need to Know

- Dogs give off calming signals to keep the peace.
- Humans unknowingly do things that stress dogs, and the dogs try to tell us not to.
- Be aware of your dog's signals to avoid potential problems.
- Humans can use dog signals to communicate with dogs and avoid conflicts.

Knowing Your Dog's Signals

In This Chapter

- Determining whether your dog is stressed
- Managing stressful situations
- Setting your dog up to succeed
- Avoiding potential problems by watching your dog

By always keeping an eye on your dog and heeding the multitude of signals he's giving you about his emotional state, you can avoid potential problems. If you ignore a dog's fear signals and pressure him, he will not only learn to fear things (and react by either aggressing or running away), he will also lose his language because it's being ignored—it doesn't "work" anymore.

Watching for Signs of Stress

If your dog is stressed and you don't know it, you might instead believe that you have a stupid or stubborn dog because of her behavior. She may be nervous about a new location or new people, but you believe that she's being "bad" when she ignores you. So you end up jerking her around and, in effect, punishing her for being afraid.

It's a dangerous thing when a dog loses her ability to tell you that she's anxious. Without the means to give off the early warning signs (also called calming signals) of nervousness, a dog is more likely to go directly to the more serious aspects of warning—growling and biting.

Learn to read your dog for signs of stress. If a child or stranger is approaching and your dog exhibits early signs of stress (lip licking, head turning, backing away, and so on), don't allow the person to approach any closer. Allowing a person to continue to approach will either put the dog into a more defensive posture or cause her to be more afraid and try to run away.

Growling

A growl is an important mode of communication from the dog to you. It's not aggression—it's a warning. When the police say, "Stop or I'll shoot," it doesn't mean they want to shoot you; it's a warning.

If you punish a dog for growling, you deny yourself a warning that your dog is feeling threatened. If you're smart, you'll thank your dog for growling because he's just letting you know that he's very uncomfortable, and if you don't stop what you're doing, he may bite you. A growling dog doesn't want to bite you—that's why he's growling as a warning.

Don't Punish the Warning Signs!

Dogs learn by association. If you punish a dog for growling, he learns to associate the bad feeling from the punishment with that—be it another dog, person, or child. The dog already felt some anxiety or fear about that object to start with, and now your punishment made him even more fearful.

If you haven't done anything to train an alternative behavior or *desensitize* the dog to that object, the next time he comes in contact with that object, those bad feelings will occur again—perhaps stronger this time. The dog will be even more anxiety-ridden in the presence of that stimulus and will feel an even greater need to be defensive. But now he can't even tell you because you punished him for giving his warning signs. And because he was punished for growling, he may go directly to biting without a warning.

MUTTLEY MEANINGS

Desensitization or **systematic desensitization** is a form of counter-conditioning in which a phobic (scared) subject (human or animal) is subjected to low levels of the frightening stimulus while relaxed. The level of frightening stimulus is gradually increased, but never at a rate to cause distress. Eventually, the fear dissipates.

If the dog is growling at you, please, please, *pretty please* don't take it personally. Your dog is just telling you that he doesn't like what you're doing. There may be an underlying cause—physical or mental—of the growling. Perhaps you hurt him inadvertently or he has a boo-boo that you didn't see.

Make sure there's no hidden reason, and then use the growl as a wake-up call that you need to avoid that situation or (if that's not possible) train the dog to accept whatever made him unhappy. If you see these signs, you must desensitize and *countercondition* your dog to any *provoking stimuli*.

MUTTLEY MEANINGS

Counterconditioning is the use of classical conditioning to reverse the unwanted effects of prior conditioning.

Provoking stimuli are things that your dog is afraid of. These can include people, dogs, cows, horses, fence posts, drainpipes, petting in inappropriate ways, the vacuum cleaner—basically anything that makes the dog nervous.

Stopping Bad Behaviors in Stressful Situations

You can (and should) stop bad behaviors before they start or escalate. It's extremely important to learn to detect the subtle signals of stress and to intervene on your dog's behalf. Waiting to do something until your dog is in full defense mode is counterproductive. Dogs in defense mode are aroused, their heart rate is high, their *adrenaline* and *glucocorticoid* levels are high, and it takes two to six days for these stress hormones to come down to normal levels. Until then, the dog is incapable of learning.

MUTTLEY MEANINGS

Adrenaline and **glucocorticoids** are hormones produced in mammals during stress to help the body prepare for a fight-or-flight response.

Any added stressor that the dog comes into contact with before the hormone levels go back to normal will set the dog's stress clock even higher, and the dog may react even more vehemently.

Strange People Approaching Your Dog

If a stranger approaches you and your dog, and your dog gets nervous, tell the other person to stop his or her approach, or simply walk away from the person. The general public doesn't own your dog, and no law I know of states that they must be allowed to pet your dog.

POOCH POINTERS

Some people might insist on approaching your nervous dog, perhaps saying, "Oh, it's okay, I have dogs at home," or some other such nonsense. It's up to you, the owner, to keep your dog safe from people like this. You wouldn't allow a stranger to approach and touch your child, would you? Of course not. So don't allow strangers to approach, especially when your dog has already shown that he's nervous.

There is some old wives' tale that says you must reach out a hand to let the dog sniff you, and after that, it is okay for you to pet him on the head. Like most old wives' tales, this is wrong! As you have learned, the dog sees this as threatening. The proper thing to do is to crouch down to the dog's level and let him sniff you at his own pace.

Dog-to-Dog Confrontations

Let dogs give their signals to each other, rather than forcing "obedience." If your dog is nervous about another dog, don't force her to walk close to the other dog—arc around at a distance so that both dogs feel comfortable.

Proper greeting etiquette from the human.
(Photo by P. Dennison)

Not every dog has to be friends with every other dog. My preference is that my dogs be calm around all other dogs, rather than expect playmates in all the dogs we meet. After all, we don't like every person we meet, either.

Leashes

You can inadvertently teach your dog to be aggressive by the way you use your leash. You should use the leash as a safety net, not as a tool. Your relationship is what should control the dog. Leashes can break or be yanked out of your hand, and collars break, too. If you use the leash as a tool, you really don't have a relationship with your dog.

If you continually yank on your dog, then you're stressing her and she can't concentrate on anything other than "What is this pressure on my neck? Stop yanking me!" She then may *redirect* onto the next object she sees.

MUTTLEY MEANINGS

Redirect or **redirected aggression** means to take an emotion that a dog or human can't express in a situation and direct it toward another object, human, or dog. For example, your mom just yelled at you, so to alleviate the stress you're feeling, you yell at anyone it is "safe" to yell at.

A dog on a leash, just by virtue of being confined, is in a defensive mode—she can't escape danger and she knows it. That's why so many dogs are aggressive when they're on a leash.

If you yank your dog away from another dog, the state of arousal becomes higher and higher until what perhaps started as a simple, "Hi, who are you, and what's your name?" quickly becomes, "Come any closer and I'll rip your throat out!" If your dog doesn't yet walk on a loose leash around other dogs, avoid the company of other dogs until you've trained more. You can certainly do some off-leash work if the other dogs are friendly and the area is safe. See Chapter 10 for a full discussion of training your dog on the leash.

DOGGIE DATA

When I was a groomer, a lovely, well-adjusted, happy Springer Spaniel, who came in often, suddenly started growling at me, and his eyes were very scary. When his owners came to pick him up, I explained what had happened and asked about any changes in the household, diet, or health. They'd also noticed a slight change in the dog's behavior, and, upon further examination, learned that the new babysitter was abusing both the dog and their grandson.

The moral? Don't ever punish your dog for growling—listen to what he's saying. I knew that the aggressive display was out of character. Because I didn't let it go, the dog and child were saved from a bad situation.

The best way to introduce dogs to each other is in a safe, enclosed area with leashes off and only two dogs at a time. A great deal of tension travels down the leash from you right to the dog. If you're nervous, the dog will be nervous and stressed about the other dog, too.

Better Ways of Coping with Stress

Fearful behaviors are self-reinforcing because those behaviors keep the scary thing away. If the beginning stages of fear don't keep the scary thing away, the level of fear will increase into aggression or avoidance until the behavior (from the dog's point of view) is successful in protecting her.

The best thing you can do is teach your dog alternative behaviors to being nervous. Teach him basic obedience, such as attention, eye contact, loose-leash walking, interactive play with you, name recognition, coming when you call, or even just standard pet tricks. Anything that keeps the dog from obsessing about the feared object counts.

Getting Out of a Bad Situation

In the beginning, if the dog is already in a frenzy, get him out of the situation. If you can catch him before he goes berserk, you can learn to calm him down without getting frustrated and without accidentally reinforcing the dog. Accidental reinforcement of bad behaviors is probably the most common cause of behavioral problems in dogs. That's why it's so important to be able to read your dog and set him up to be right.

Human Body Postures That Calm

When you become fluent in "dog," you'll be able to stop the behavior almost before it starts. Here are some ways to calm a dog using your body and her language:

- Put the dog in an area where there are no prey objects or other stress-inducing stimuli in the dog's line of sight or hearing.

- Stand upright, facing the same direction as the dog. You can also turn your back on the dog or just twist your body away.

- Avoid eye contact, unless the dog is seeking your eye contact—then acknowledge her glance calmly, momentarily. If you've taught her that calm eye contact gets her what she wants, so much the better. You can then blink your eyes, avert your gaze, or turn your head away.

A person turning her body to avoid the dog.
(Photo by P. Dennison)

A person turning her head to avoid looking at the dog as the dog jumps.
(Photo by P. Dennison)

- Speak in a soft and calm voice, or be silent—silence is best. You can also yawn or lick your lips.

- Move calmly and slowly, or freeze in position.

- Pet the dog, but be sure to pet along the back and sides in long, soothing strokes with a very light touch.

Setting the Dog Up for Success

If your dog shows signs of fear or nervousness (review the signs in Chapter 5), don't set him up to be fearful. Limit his access to the feared objects, and slowly, methodically go in closer while reinforcing for calm behaviors.

Watch Your Dog Carefully

If your dog is nervous about inanimate objects—swing sets, rowboats, plastic reindeer, and the like—don't laugh; just stand still while he makes a fool of himself. You can place treats all around the object and let the dog move closer at his own pace.

If your dog is nervous about having company over, put her in a separate room until you can take the time to train her to accept company. If your dog jumps on people coming to the door, put her on leash while you open the door and reinforce her for sitting. If she has problems with kids and bikes going past the picture window, close the curtains.

If your dog doesn't like petting on the head (99 percent of dogs don't like it), then, until you train him to like it, don't pet him on the head. Think your dog does? Try this test: call him over to you and pet him on the head. If he avoids your touch, ducks his head, moves away completely, or moves his head toward your hand (as if to bite—even without a show of teeth), well, guess what? Your dog is part of the ninety-ninth percentile and is completely normal.

DOGGIE DATA

Louise came in with her dog, Teddy, with her arms bloody and scratched. Teddy didn't like petting at all and would tell her so in a not-nice way. After one week of working with Teddy, he allowed Louise to pet him. We taught him to enjoy petting by pairing a light touch with treats. After the second week, Teddy was actively enjoying having Louise pet him. (See more about the Premack Principle in Chapter 13.)

Can you teach your dogs to accept inappropriate behaviors from strangers, and inappropriate handling by veterinarians? Of course you can, and you *must!* It's important to remember, though, that dogs don't naturally like certain behaviors and you should handle them as you would handle any behavior that isn't natural for a dog—*train them!* Specific guidelines for teaching your dog to accept handling are addressed in Chapter 8.

Until you can take the time to train your dog to accept the human world in all its complexities, manage the situations as best you can so that your dog doesn't practice nervous or fearful behaviors. After all, practice makes perfect, whether the behavior is "good" or "bad."

A dog trained to accept threatening body postures from humans.
(Photo by J. Killion)

Get Your Dog's Attention

When you want to attract your dog away from something else more interesting, think like prey. Dogs are attracted to movement because they're predators! Here's what to do:

- Your body posture should be low to the ground and you should approach sideways. Be careful not to loom over the dog because this is perceived as aggressive. You can lean backward, wave your arms, wiggle your fingers, or run away.

- Avoid direct eye contact or give a sideways glance.

- Use a high-pitched, excited, squeaky voice, or even a whistle. Loud, deep voices do the opposite—they repel dogs.

- Move side to side or away from the dog—the faster the better. Move right and left—act really excited!

- Play with whatever toys your dog really likes.

- You can do some mild roughhousing with the dog to energize, but not to overstimulate her.

What else can you do to ensure that your dog grows up with a healthy attitude in this complex world we live in? You can educate yourself, your family, and your friends about canine behavior and body language. You can get the pups out and about, as much as possible, from the time they're eight weeks old, always moving at their pace and their comfort level. You can teach your puppies manners and acceptance of the human species they now live with. You can always observe, watch over, and listen to your dog—in his or her language.

Pop Quiz

1. Why is it *not* a good idea to punish your dog for growling?

2. Why do many dogs act differently when on leash than when off leash?

3. Name a few ways you can calm your dog down if she is stressed.

4. If your dog doesn't like petting, what should you do?

The Least You Need to Know

- Watch your dog at all times for signs of stress or fear—and *do not* punish these signs.
- Learn to manage your dog's stressful situations, such as meeting other dogs and people, and being on a leash.
- Use your leash as a safety net, not to drag your dog around.
- Learn and watch for your dog's calming signals to avoid problems.

What You and Your Dog Need to Know

In This Chapter

- Starting with a good relationship
- Things to do before you start training
- Teaching your dog to stare at you adoringly
- Come to me, baby!

Before you start training in earnest, you and your dog must master certain things together. This chapter discusses the importance of building a relationship with your dog before you start asking her to learn the behaviors you want. After you've done that, you can work toward starting your training sessions by teaching eye contact and priming the clicker. Then you can teach your dog the all-important "Come" command.

Let's Work on Your Relationship

Ninety-nine percent of all dog training is building your relationship and learning to read your dog (as discussed in Chapter 5). The other 1 percent is the actual obedience and manners stuff. Try to get the manners without the relationship and you won't succeed.

Just Say No to "No"

The first step is to stop all negativity. Drop all physical and verbal punishments, including the word "*no*," and any other words you come up with that mean "no." "*No*" very easily escalates into a screamed "*NO!*" which dredges up some very negative emotion from us, which is then transmitted to the dog. Remember—classical conditioning happens 24 hours a day, 7 days a week, whether you want it to or not. You just can't get away from Pavlov!

Look at it this way. "No" is not a verb. Verbs are our friends! No doesn't tell the dog what you want him to do instead. "No" does nothing positive. Imagine living with someone who is always nitpicking, screaming at you, hitting you. After a while you may just give up because nothing you do is right. Same with your dog. Focus on what he's doing right and you'll all be happier.

DOGGIE DATA

Positive training might very well change your life as well as your dog's. Sally and John brought their Golden Retriever pup for training. After six weeks of diligently practicing each week, they told me that they actually stopped saying "No" to each other! Another client, Henry, was a very sullen, negative person with job-related problems and two very nice mixed-breed puppies. After training with me for a few weeks, he mentioned that positively training his dogs had turned his life around. He started to treat his co-workers in a more positive manner and was doing a better job at work. The best part is that everyone on the job noticed and complimented him on his change of attitude.

Focusing on the Good Stuff!

Too often we reinforce the dog by paying attention to her when she's doing something "bad" (such as eating the chair, or anything else you've decided is unacceptable), and we never notice the 23 hours a day that she's actually doing good things. If you pay attention to the dog only when she's bad, then she will do only bad things. This is called handler-induced bad behaviors (see Chapter 17). When she's lying down or being quiet or whatever you deem as appropriate behavior—*praise* her! If you can't watch her and you know she will soon be driving you crazy, then just put her in her crate before she starts practicing any bad behaviors.

Don't use putting the dog in his crate as a punishment. The dog needs to see the crate as a safe, secure haven—especially if he has to be in there at night or during the day. You can throw in a toy or a treat, so that the crate isn't seen as a punishment. Putting the dog away *after* a bad behavior happens does not teach the dog anything. Next time, watch his signals more closely and put him away before he gets out of control.

POOCH POINTERS

There are four magic words to use instead of "no": "come," "sit," "stay," and "give." When your dog has learned what these behaviors mean, use them instead. If your dog has her paws up on the counter, "come" works well. If your dog is digging through the garbage, "come-sit-give" are the words you should use. I don't even use the words "leave it," because that's too much like "no." "Come" works better because it gives the dog more direction.

Communing with Nature

Don't underestimate the value of taking your dog to a park, sitting on a park bench, and just hangin' out. On very hot days or days I'm just feeling lazy, I'll pack up the dogs in the van, go someplace pretty, green, and shady, and just hang out with each dog, one at a time. That way, they all get some "alone" time with me.

I add massage along with petting and we watch the world go by, as I thank my lucky stars I am working at a job that enables me to do this! Any fun or relaxing thing you share with your dog builds up some nice money in the bank account of your relationship.

Getting Started with Training

Before you can start any training, your dog needs to know a few things. You need to make the click sound valuable and meaningful, and you need to teach him that eye contact with you, hearing his name, and "come," are worth a million bucks. You cannot positively train a dog if he is not focused on you.

First Things First

First of all, start your session by priming the clicker to remind your dog that "click" means food. Count out at least 60 treats and, with the dog in front of you, follow these steps:

1. Click the clicker.

2. Hand your dog one treat within a half second after the click (this is the optimum timing—after three seconds the dog won't make the proper association that click means food).

3. Repeat for at least two minutes.

You shouldn't have to do this for more than two minutes. If your dog doesn't make the connection right away, don't think that you have a lemon—just do it longer. Some dogs may be nervous about strange new noises, so just in case your dog is one of those, put the clicker in your pocket to muffle the sound at first. If your dog runs away in fear the first time you click, don't use the clicker! Just use a "yes" as your click word.

Look into My Eyes

In the same training session (after priming the clicker), you are going to teach the dog to stare at you adoringly. Without eye contact, you can't teach the dog anything, so this is the next step in training.

Again, have a handful of treats ready and the dog in front of you. Now follow these steps:

1. Wait for eye contact. Your dog will probably mug your hand, so, if needed, put your hands behind your back. Keep your eyes on your dog and just wait silently.

2. Be ready to click and treat. Usually after 3 to 10 seconds, your dog will accidentally look up at your face.

3. Stand still and wait again. The next time your dog looks at you, click and treat. On average, it takes dogs two to three minutes to figure out where the "magic button" is (looking at your face).

Repeat for a minute or two every day for two weeks and then a few times a week for the rest of the dog's life. You might have noticed that I haven't asked you to name this (eye contact). That is because it isn't necessary. Just train for it and your dog will be boring holes in your head automatically. If you name it, the dog will only look at you when you say your "look at me" cue.

Making eye contact.
(Photo by P. Dennison)

My Name Is "No, No, Bad Dog!" —What's Yours?

Does your dog know her name? Or if she does, does she think that hearing her name is a bad thing? Here is the fastest, easiest, most surefire way to teach your dog that her name is valuable and something to respond to instantly (again, borrowing from Pavlov—name means reinforcement):

1. Have a few treats in your hand or pocket.

2. When the dog gives you eye contact, say her name.

3. Then click and treat.

Repeat for 5 to 10 minutes every day for 2 weeks and then a few times a week for the rest of the dog's life.

In the beginning stages, be sure not to use the dog's name to get her to look at you—say her name *after* she looks at you. One way is nagging, the other is teaching. After a day or two, you should start to see the dog get whiplash looking at you when you say her name. If you just rescued your dog or you have truly poisoned your dog's name, this is the perfect time to change your dog's name.

CANINE CAVEATS

You can very easily train your dog to ignore his name. Say that your dog is out in the yard and you want him in the house. You call his name. He ignores you. You continue to call his name repeatedly. Each time you yell it louder and louder and louder, hoping he will finally answer you. Guess what? He won't, and now he'll ignore his name whenever you use it. You can even do this with "come" as well! Yippee!

To continue to keep eye contact strong, every time you say the dog's name and she responds, reinforce her! "Good! You responded when I said your name! Brilliant doggie!" Be sure to heavily reinforce, especially when there are distractions around—then really go crazy and make her think that she won a million dollars worth of treats at a slot machine.

Dogs Don't Know What "Good Dog" Means

To drive up the value of your praise words (remember, these words are not naturally reinforcing for your dog), pair the words with food. You don't have to click for this one. You're turning your praise words into a marker signal—just as you did with the clicker.

> **POOCH POINTERS**
>
> You can even make your smile a reinforcer. I do this because I can't bring food into the obedience ring, so I use a smile as a reward. If the judges ever make us wear paper bags over our heads during competition, I'm in big trouble.

To make your words into reinforcements, follow the preceding steps for priming the clicker. Say your praise word(s)—"good dog," "wahoo," "yippee," "excellent," and so on—and then treat within a half second. If you use many different ones (as I do), then say one word per session.

Because we talk to and around our dogs, and dogs are not a verbal species, speech tends to become white noise to them. You need to do this exercise for more than two minutes (as we did with the clicker). Continue to pair the praise word with food a few times per day for a few weeks.

I'd Rather Eat Poop: "Come"

The most important thing you can teach your dog is to come reliably when called (also known as a *recall*). This behavior could save his life one day, so please don't skimp on the training. The first step to building a reliable "come" is to continue to build your relationship, and be variable and unpredictable in how you reinforce his behavior.

The hardest thing that you're up against is learning to become more interesting than the environment. It takes creativity, patience, perseverance, and management. If your dog doesn't have a reliable recall, then don't let him off the leash in an unprotected area.

Step 1: Using Classical Conditioning

Start training your dog to come with these steps:

1. Have a few treats in your hand and have the dog in front of you.

2. When the dog gives you eye contact, say his name, then say, "Come."

3. Click and treat.

4. Repeat for a minute or two (20 times) every day for two weeks and then a few times a week for the rest of the dog's life.

In this session, you don't expect the dog to actually move out of position. You just want him to listen to the words. If your dog has a history of ignoring the word "come," feel free to change your word. "Here" is a popular recall word.

Recall the "basic recipe":

- For this behavior alone, do not phase out the food or other reinforcers—*ever*—for the life of the dog. Reinforcers can be petting, praise, food, or a rousing game of tug. Whatever the dog loves, do them all!

- Make your "come" signal distinct (not sometimes "c'mere," sometimes "come," sometimes "here," sometimes "let's go," and so on). In the beginning stages of the recall, don't say the word unless your dog is already on his way to you! You *must* pair the word with the behavior for the dog to learn exactly what "come" means.

- Say "come" only when you're prepared to reinforce heavily— for at least 20 seconds! If you don't have anything on you, you can run to the reinforcers, all the while keeping his attention on you.

- Make sure the dog comes within a few inches—do not reach out to feed the dog.

- Make sure that when you say "come" it doesn't sound like this: "Comecomecomecome—come." To the dog's ear that sounds different from "come," so your cue will be confusing.

CANINE CAVEATS

Be sure to use the word "come" only for a recall. Don't dilute it by using it for loose-leash walking or anything else.

Whistle Training

You can also add using a whistle as your "come *now!*" recall cue. The sound of the whistle *never* has an angry or annoyed tone, never changes inflection, never changes in sound. Whistle training also works well for older dogs who may be starting to lose their hearing.

To do this, repeat the previous steps and, instead of saying your verbal "come" word, blast your whistle (Step One). I recommend two short blasts and one really long blast, and then treat. (You don't have to use the clicker for this.) I recommend two short and one long blast because if your dog gets loose on a windy night or there are other loud noises around, the sound will travel better and she will hear this progression better than just one or two short blasts. (See Appendix B for the *Training the Whistle Recall* DVD.)

For two solid weeks, just whistle-treat, whistle-treat. Do it in one- to two-minute sessions (or until you pass out from lack of oxygen). You want the dog to have a conditioned response to the whistle, in that it takes no thought on their part, they just react.

Step 2: Playing Hide-and-Seek

Have someone hold your dog while you run away and hide. Then call the dog. The instant you say the dog's name ("Fluffy, come"), your helper should drop the leash. You can also do this and whistle instead of saying "come." When the dog finds you, have a huge party with all sorts of reinforcers.

Just as you won't call your dog in the beginning stages of training the recall, don't whistle unless you know for a fact that your dog is on her way. Otherwise your dog will learn to ignore the whistle.

A person dropping the leash as the owner calls the dog.
(Photo by P. Dennison)

Or if you're alone, just run and hide while the dog is in another room, and then call her. I do this with my dogs—it's pretty funny with four dogs in a teeny tiny house all skidding around trying to get to me first.

Step 3: Walking in a Field or Trail

Bring your fanny pack, some toys and treats, and a long leash. *Before* the dog gets to the end of the line, say his name—once. You don't want his name associated with a painful pop on the collar, which is why you do it before he hits the end of the leash. Better still if you put a harness on him to avoid any tracheal, spinal, or neck damage.

POOCH POINTERS

If your dog doesn't respond, just stand still and wait. If needed, turn your back to the dog and wait. You can even try squatting down. She'll eventually come to you, and when she does, click once and reward heavily with all types of reinforcers.

If he responds by turning his head to you, say, "Come," or whistle. When he comes to you, click once and treat heavily. You can even run backward, enticing him to come to you. (Be sure that you don't yank him by the collar.) Continue to practice this as you continue your walk. If he doesn't respond to his name, then don't say it again right now. Wait until you really think he will respond—this would not be when his entire head is down in a gopher hole.

Step 4: The Drop-the-Cookie-and-Run-Like-Heck Game

This is a wonderful "come" game that both you and the dog will love. And you get to continue to build that positive relationship because all these training exercises are *fun!* Follow these steps:

1. Throw a cookie a few feet away. (Make sure the dog sees it!)

2. Tell your dog, "Get it!"

3. Run away fast!

4. As the dog is coming to you, say, "Come," or whistle (pairing the word or sound with the behavior).

5. When she gets to you, click and treat with a *jackpot*.

 MUTTLEY MEANINGS

A **jackpot** is lots of treats given to the dog, one at a time. I like to give a jackpot when the dog has done something hard for the very first time, or if a behavior is particularly wonderful.

Jackpots are given for every "come," and are fed one cookie at a time. To a dog, a wad of food is the same as one cookie, so spread them out and keep the dog with you longer! Be variable in the number of cookies in the jackpots. Add in lots of play, petting, and praise as reinforcers.

Build up your reinforcement history and your dog will remember just how generous you are, especially when it really matters! Two to three treats is *not* a jackpot. When I heavily reinforce a recall, I am using 10 to 30 treats!

You don't want the dog to get used to taking one cookie and then running away from you because he knows you pay out only one cookie. One day he'll be distracted by something more interesting than your one cookie, such as a squirrel. Chasing that squirrel could lead him into the path of a truck.

You should also do this exercise without running. Just throw the treat farther away and wait for the dog to get it. When she finds the treat, call or whistle her to you. You want to vary this with running away because otherwise your dog will think that the recall signal is you running away.

This is a *super* game to play with all family members in a big circle—kind of a "round robin" game. The dogs love it, the kids love it, and the dogs get really tired. And everyone knows that a tired dog is a good dog!

Dropping the cookie ...
(Photo by P. Dennison)

... and running like heck (and calling your dog to "come" as he is coming).
(Photo by P. Dennison)

Step 5: Adding Distractions

Get yourself a 50-foot line and practice, in tons of locations where
there are distractions, all of the "come" behaviors that were just
described. The long line becomes a portable fence! You can't exercise
a dog properly on a six-foot leash, and I don't use leashes as tools.
Leashes are to be used as safety nets only.

The heavier the distractions, the larger and more exciting your reinforcers should be. Start with small distractions that are far away, and gradually build to greater ones that are closer.

You can practice this method with many distractions—not all, of course. You don't want to allow your dog to chase cars, but you can still train an instant recall for when he's aroused by using "safe" and highly valued distractions. Although your dog loves to chase cars, he also loves to chase balls or Frisbees, so you can use his high arousal to toys (instead of speeding cars) to train for instant recall. Teach your dog to come off a toy in the midst of chasing it by following these steps:

1. Have the dog off-leash in a safe area, or on a 50-foot line with it dragging. Start off with the very lowest valued item you can think of, such as a paper towel tube.

2. Throw the tube.

3. Tell the dog, "Get it!"

4. As the dog goes toward it—just a step or two—call or whistle him back to you and heavily reward him with toys he likes, petting, praise, or food.

5. Throw the tube again and repeat a few times until he's running back to you at top speed.

6. Now find another item, slightly more valued than the tube. Repeat the exercise, always rewarding heavily for the recall. Gradually increase the value of the thrown toy while increasing the value of your rewards when he comes back to you.

7. If at any point your dog ignores you and ends up getting the toy, don't say anything—just stand there passively, count to five, and start over. Don't block the dog or become a barrier.

This is not about obedience. ("How *dare* she not come back to me?") This is about building your relationship, so that your dog *wants* to play this game with you, and *wants* to come off a toy, bike, car, deer, because playing with you is *fun* to do.

A Border Collie coming away from a tennis ball.
(Photo by J. Guz)

Continue in short sessions—three to five throws of the object per session—until you're using the highest-valued toy imaginable and your dog is making skid marks in the grass to come back to you. Periodically, allow her to get to the toy without calling her back to you, play with her with the toy, and then work your recall again. The more recall practice you can do with safe objects when the dog is aroused, the more easily she will come off inappropriate objects when in that same state.

Pop Quiz

1. Why is the word "no" useless? What should you say instead?

2. Have you trained your dog (in the past) to ignore his name or "come" cue? If so, what is your new "come" word?

3. Why is it a good idea *not* to name the behavior of eye contact?

4. In the beginning stages, why is it a good idea *not* to call your dog or whistle unless she is already on her way to you?

5. If your dog comes away from something really interesting (such as a squirrel or deer), even if it is 10 minutes later, what should you do?

The Least You Need to Know

- The basis of good training is first building a positive relationship with your dog.
- Before you can start training, you must prime the clicker, master eye contact and name recognition, and build praise-word recognition.
- Teaching your dog to come when called is important in later training and could one day save his or her life.
- Have fun with your dog—continue to add to the piggy bank of your relationship.

Positive Puppy Socialization

In This Chapter

- Hello, world—socialization basics
- Don't touch!—getting your dog used to being touched
- Do I know you?
- It's a big, scary world out there

Puppies are like little sponges—they soak up whatever you teach them. It's your job to make sure all of those early associations are good ones. I've worked with many eight-week-old puppies and they very rapidly learn proper behaviors without the use of punishment.

This chapter is devoted to socialization and the things you need to do to make sure your puppy grows into a confident adult. If you don't have time to do these things for your puppy, you might want to rethink owning a dog. It's your responsibility to "bring up Baby" correctly and humanely. If you practice socialization—getting your dog accustomed to petting, handling, meeting strangers, and being polite around food and the food bowl—you and your dog will live happily ever after.

These methods are also great when working with rescued dogs. If you've started out using punishment-based methods and want to switch to positive, never fear! Dogs are resilient and you can turn them around.

Social(ization) Studies

The optimum puppy age for early *socialization* is 8 to 20 weeks. Any time after that and you'll be dealing with *counterconditioning* and *desensitization*, because you've lost your window of opportunity.

Everyone says that you should properly socialize your new pup, but no one tells you exactly how to go about it. Because socialization is so vitally important to your dog's future mental and emotional well-being and outlook on life, it's imperative to start your new pup off on the right paw. Please be aware that "early" doesn't mean "only." If you only take advantage of early socialization and then think you're done—you're not. Socialization should continue until the dog is two years of age.

 MUTTLEY MEANINGS

Socialization involves the controlled introduction of various situations and things so that the dog develops positive associations with them.

As your puppy gets older, she will develop new fears. One day she'll be fine with something or someone, and the next day she'll be terrified. These are called fear periods.

The typical ages for fear periods are 8 to 10 weeks of age, then 16 to 20 weeks, at approximately 6 months of age, and again around 10 months of age. Fear periods return at around 14 to 18 months. It's *vital* that you don't laugh at, scold, or comfort the dog during fear periods. Keep them relatively isolated during these times and introduce them to *nothing new*. They are vulnerable during these fear periods, so by all means, keep them home and safe for a week or so. You'll know when they come back to normal and you can then resume taking them out and about. Ignore and wait for calm behaviors that you can then reinforce. If you pressure a puppy during a fear period, she will have that fear for life.

Some people may think that socializing a dog means indiscriminately dragging her around to new locations or having strangers walk up and invasively pet her. This may very well lead to behavior problems later, such as fear or aggression. Proper socialization is actually a controlled introduction of various situations and things so that the dog develops positive associations with them.

Bull Mastiff puppy with a dumbbell.
(Photo by P. Dennison)

Socialization is about exposing your puppy and adolescent dog gradually and systematically to different types of people, places, things, surfaces, noises, touch (from you and strangers), other dogs, and other species of animals. Socialization is all about setting the dog up for success—introducing her to each new situation in such a manner that she won't be afraid. The goal is to build confidence and trust.

Watch Your Puppy for Signs of Stress

The most important aspect of training is detecting signs of stress and fear in your puppy. If you don't recognize these signs, you may be pushing the dog into situations that he can't deal with and may be creating more fear, aggression, or anxiety about a specific place/person/species. (See Chapters 5 and 6 for the observable signs of stress.)

If your dog exhibits any of these signs, you may be pushing your socialization sessions too fast or for too long.

Places for Socialization

What will your dog have to feel comfortable with during his lifetime? He'll visit the veterinarian and groomer, where strangers will handle him in sometimes very uncomfortable ways. You'll want to take your dog to the park, to new and different places, and into and out of strange doorways. You'll also want him to be comfortable going to the kennel. He'll also need to feel comfortable with strangers going in and out of your house.

The dog will need to feel comfortable walking on different types of surfaces such as concrete, gravel, linoleum, carpet, wood or tile floors, grass, snow, puddles, mud, and ice. You need to build his confidence in going up and down all different types of stairs, jumping into the car on his own (especially useful if you have a large-breed dog), riding in the car, and walking along a busy street. Your dog needs to get used to seeing or hearing men in hats or with beards, people in wheelchairs, kids on skateboards, umbrellas, babies crying, kids playing, bicycles, loud music and other sounds, cars driving by, other dogs—the list is endless!

CANINE CAVEATS

Children and adults will undoubtedly come up to your dog and want to pet her. In this litigious society, it's important to get in touch with your pet's state of mind when you expose her to others. It's also important to teach strangers the correct way to approach your dog.

Kennels and Vets

There will come a time when you'll need to board your dog (at a reputable kennel, please—get many references and check them out). Don't wait until you're actually going on vacation to teach the dog to like the kennel. Start by leaving him for an hour with yummy treats and plenty of chew toys. Repeat many times, gradually increasing the time he stays in the kennel. If an hour is too much for your pup, start at five minutes and slowly build the duration of time that he can be without you comfortably.

You should also have this type of short, trial visit to the vet, to prepare for actual vet check-ups. Bring treats and toys, hang out for a little while, and then go home. Repeat many times. Many vets will even allow you to put your dog up on a table (scary, slippery, high up), and the vet will pet them. Believe me, they'll be thrilled you are taking the time now, because that means less problems for them later on!

To Home School or Not to Home School

You can and should start your puppy in Puppy K as soon as possible. My preference is about eight to nine weeks of age. They still retain immunity from the first set of puppy shots and their minds are wide open to learning new things. You have the added benefit of fewer experiences in their lives that have created problems: with other dogs, strangers, new sights and sounds, handling, house training, nipping, and so on. As with all training classes, be sure to observe first before signing up.

Many vets still think that you should keep your puppy in "house arrest" until they are five to six months old. The problem with that is the window for socialization is from 8 to 16 or 20 weeks. When closed, it can never be opened again and you may have a real problem later on. See Appendix B for the link to an article by the American Veterinary Society of Animal Behavior for the correct timing of Puppy K.

Is One Class Enough?

Go to school numerous times! I mean it! The average puppy kinder-garten lasts from six to eight weeks. Don't expect your puppy to be thoroughly socialized with other dogs for the rest of his life in such a short time. See what the school offers in terms of additional train-ing levels. I personally offer Advanced Puppy K (mostly off-leash), Competition Puppy (for those puppies that already have their careers laid out), agility, rally, tricks, Canine Good Citizen, Therapy Dog, and more.

In addition, you can start your own puppy play group and keep it going. Put up flyers at the vet's office, pet shops, or groomer, asking other people to bring their pups to your play group.

Even if you have other dogs at home and your puppy gets along fine, don't think this is enough. Your new puppy needs to be exposed to many other dogs in his lifetime. Be sure, however, that the puppies and older dogs you introduce him to are friendly. It would be terrible to have your puppy attacked and possibly traumatized for life, fearful of his own species.

Doing these exercises *from the day you bring the dog home* may save you a great deal of heartache later. Continue to periodically practice all of these behaviors for the life of the dog.

How About Dog Parks?

I am not a big fan of dog parks. There may be some groups out there that "interview" the dogs to make sure they are safe and will be a nice playmate for your puppy or older dog, but that isn't the norm. Not everyone is truly aware of the ability of their dog to get along with other dogs properly, or can recognize when their dog is over the top or not appropriate for that kind of situation.

I hear stories about people bringing their aggressive dog to dog parks, erroneously thinking it is the best place to socialize their dog! Yikes!

Just as you would do research for anything new in your life, be sure to go and watch first—without your dog/puppy to see how the play looks to you. See if the site is broken down into little, medium, and big dogs and observe how the dogs in each group play. You wouldn't want to bring your Maltese puppy into a group of Labs and Goldens who all play rough.

Petting and Handling

Repetition of calm behaviors is one of the building blocks to a healthy and happy relationship with your dog.

It's a dangerous world out there and it's important to recognize that uninvited hands or faces reaching down toward a dog's head can be seen, from the dog's perspective, as being aggressive. As a consequence, a large percentage of dog bites happen to children because children enthusiastically push themselves abruptly into a dog's face. You don't have to just put up with your dog's dislike of handling—you can *train* him to love it, but at the same time protect him as well.

Hard to Handle

You think your dog needs to be bathed and brushed; she thinks otherwise. She bites you or the brush, or she may not even let you get that far—she may run away at the sight of anything that even looks like a grooming implement. And toenail clipping? Forget about it!

The first step to teaching your dog how to handle unwanted attention with a minimum of stress is to begin the process of desensitization. An additional side benefit is that as you work with your dog in this way, you build a level of trust and establish a kind of communication that makes your training with her easier as you move into more advanced levels. Before starting these sessions, you must first practice the behaviors (priming the clicker, "sit," "down," "stand," and eye contact) in Chapters 7 and 9.

Simple Steps for Handling

The goal of this exercise is to reinforce *no movement* and acceptance from the dog while you touch and hold him. Start your session by giving your dog a few treats to get his attention. Break the training session into two or three sessions of approximately five minutes each. Keep your sessions short and successful—just a few minutes at a time, as many times per day as you can fit in. Be sure to include all family members in the touching sessions—not all at once, but one at a time.

Step 1. One arm around dog.
(Photo by P. Dennison)

Step 2. Both arms around dog.
(Photo by P. Dennison)

Step 3. One arm around dog, palm of hand on dog's cheek.
(Photo by P. Dennison)

Step 4. Both arms over dog so that teeth are away from vet.
(Photo by P. Dennison)

Step 5. One arm around dog, one hand under dog's chin for jugular blood draw.
(Photo by P. Dennison)

Step 6. Collar grab.
(Photo by P. Dennison)

Step 7. Lead by collar.
(Photo by P. Dennison)

Step 8. Scruff grab.
(Photo by P. Dennison)

Now follow these "basic recipe" steps. (Don't use the clicker for these—it's too cumbersome, unless you have a second person to help you.)

1. With your dog sitting or standing, place one arm around the dog. If he doesn't move, say, "Yes," and give him a treat. Repeat about five to six times.

2. Place both arms around dog. As long as he doesn't struggle, say, "Yes," and give him a treat. Repeat five to six times.

3. Place one arm around dog and with the palm of your hand, put that hand on his cheek (not his muzzle) and bring his face in toward your armpit. Say, "Yes," and treat. Repeat five to six times.

4. With the dog standing, place both arms over the dog, using your upper arm to bring his head behind you (so his teeth are away from anyone's face). Say, "Yes," if he doesn't move and give him a treat. Repeat five to six times.

5. Place one arm around dog's chest and put the palm of your other hand under his chin and lift up, move his face to the right and left, say, "Yes," if he doesn't move, treat and release. You need to practice this one just in case you ever have blood drawn from his jugular vein.

6. When he is comfortable with step 5, add in tapping his jugular (or thereabouts) to get him used to it.

A person leaning over a dog and the dog displaying a submissive reaction.
(Photo by P. Dennison)

Make sure you practice all these steps for at least two weeks and have friends help you. It is all well and good that you can handle your dog, but you need to make sure that strangers (vets) can handle your dog as well.

You may sometimes need to grab your dog's collar—leashes break, someone lets the dog out by mistake, or the dog ends up in a dangerous situation where all bets are off in terms of positive training. Teach your dog to accept these next steps and it may just save his life one day. These are *not* about scruff shakes and alpha rolls—they are about keeping your dog safe and comfortable with all types of handling.

1. Grab (gently at first) the collar, then "Yes"/treat/release. Repeat five to six times. Be sure to grab from many different directions—underneath, side, and on top. That way, if a stranger tries to grab your dog before he runs out into the street, your dog will think, "Oh goodie, cookie time!"

2. Now take hold of the collar and gently lead your dog a few feet, using a treat as a lure to start. As long as he doesn't struggle, then "Yes"/treat/release. This comes in handy when you catch the dog but forget in your panic to grab the leash.

3. The collar may slip off one day and all of a sudden you have a naked, loose dog. Practice gently grabbing his scruff/hair, say, "Yes," and treat. When he is comfortable with this, as in step 2, start to lead him while holding onto his scruff.

There are also times when you will need to check out his belly and pubic areas for fleas, ticks, and rash patrol.

Very gently, roll your puppy over and rub his belly, say, "Yes," if he doesn't resist and give him a treat. If he does resist, try to lure him over while gently pushing. This is *not* about being dominant! He should become accustomed to this pretty quickly and allow you to roll him over without incident.

The correct way to hold the clicker and food in one hand.
(Photo by P. Dennison)

Brushing

Some dogs don't like to be brushed so you'll have to teach him to like it. For the very young pup, you can slather something gooey (such as peanut butter or cream cheese) on the refrigerator and let him lick it while you gently brush or pet with a light stroke. Stop before he's done licking. You can do this in the bathtub as well. Get him used to all different kinds of things as early as possible. In addition to the previous exercises, place your hand gently along the side of the dog's face. When he's comfortable with that, you can add head touching and then slowly add in each body part: ears; tail; face; back of his neck and shoulders; each leg, foot, and toe; gums; and teeth.

If you have a breed of dog that needs regular grooming (not just a bath), you have to do some extra things. For instance, if your dog has a beard, be sure to teach him to accept you holding his beard. If your dog has hair that will grow over her eyes, you'll need to teach her to accept scissors coming toward her eyes. For this one, use your finger first, then a pencil, and then scissors. Groomers are people, too, and don't have magic wands to miraculously make your dog a pleasure to groom. Practice these things, and your groomer will thank you!

Repeat these exercises a few times per day for a few weeks, touching all body parts gently. When he likes gentle petting, you can gradually add rougher petting. You can even teach the dog to accept pinching (which is a similar sensation to getting an injection), by using this method.

POOCH POINTERS

When picking up feet, especially a back one, remember that dogs don't naturally know how to stand on three legs. Place your other hand gently under her belly to give her some support. After the pup gets the hang of it, you won't need to help her from falling over.

Be careful and go slowly. If you let go, you are reinforcing the struggling. If you don't let go, you may freak him out. The best course is to go slowly enough so that the dog *likes* being handled. Redirect with a treat if needed. The key here is to slowly build up to complete body touching so that the dog wouldn't even think about moving away.

Supporting the dog to keep his balance while holding his back leg up.
(Photo by P. Dennison)

This may take quite a few sessions depending on how sensitive your pup is to handling. Don't rush, and don't get angry—these emotions will get you in trouble later.

CANINE CAVEATS

I mean it. If you're nervous, squeamish, or not sure exactly where the "quick" (the blood supply to the nail) is, don't even try to clip your dog's nails. You can see the quick more easily on a dog with white nails. If your dog has black nails, you'll be working blind.

If you decide that you want to clip your dog's nails yourself, just cut off the tip of them at first. If you're nervous at all—just one iota of nervousness—do not, I repeat, *do not* clip your dog's nails. All it takes is one "Oh my god, I made you bleed!" while you run around screaming hysterically, to turn your dog into a toenail demon. You can still teach the dog to accept this and leave the actual clipping to a professional.

Doggie Food Bowls

If you don't train your dog to be calm around food bowls, you may be asking for food-guarding issues later on. Skip these exercises and you'd better fill up your first-aid kit! Follow these steps:

CANINE CAVEATS

Please don't think that these behaviors aren't important "because my last dog didn't have any of these issues." It's 10,000 times easier to teach proper behavior from the beginning than to try to fix it later after a problem surfaces.

1. Hand your dog a bowl with a few pieces of food in it.

2. When she's done eating, take the bowl away and give her another one with a few pieces of food in it.

3. Repeat bunches of times—15 to 20 times.

Now comes the second step:

1. Hand your dog a bowl with a few pieces of food in it.

2. Before she's done eating, lower your hand to the bowl and add more food to it.

3. Repeat bunches of times—20 to 25 times over the course of a few days.

Now for the third step with the food bowl:

1. Hand your dog a bowl with a few pieces of food in it.

2. Before she's done eating, gently remove the food bowl *at the exact same time that you hand her another bowl with a few pieces of food in it.*

3. Repeat these steps 30 to 50 times over the course of a few days.

Make it *fun* for your dog—make it *more* reinforcing when you take the food bowl away than when she keeps it to herself. You can always add more food in the second bowl than you did in the first bowl.

Stranger Danger

Progressing to the next stage, acclimating the dog to strangers, start by allowing your dog to observe strangers from a distance. Later you let her get closer to people and have them touch her. Your dog may be fine the first time out, but behavior is not static, and what she is comfortable with now may freak her out later during a fear period.

From a Distance

Go to a place where there are just a few people and few distractions, staying approximately 50 to 100 feet away. As the dog continues to remain calm, you can gradually go in closer.

If your dog is frightened and tries to back up or run away, *do not* say, "It's okay, it's okay!" or console her in any way. Consoling a dog reinforces the dog's fear because dogs don't speak English (really!). No matter what you say, you're still paying attention to the dog and rewarding the fearful behavior. The best course is to ...

1. Say *nothing!* Do nothing.

2. Stand there passively and keep your eyes on your dog.

3. When her body relaxes, praise her, and then ask her to do whatever she knows how to do ("sit," "down") and then keep her busy interacting with you.

Timing is everything—note that the praise and rewards come *after* the dog is calm and then performs another behavior. If you give the dog rewards when the dog is nervous, you are reinforcing the nervousness.

CANINE CAVEATS

It's easy to think that if your dog is frantically wagging his tail, then he's deliriously happy. A frantically wagging tail is just that—frantic. (Yes, even if your puppy is a Lab.) It's a typical puppy submissive behavior, showing stress. It's one way that a subordinate puppy approaches an adult dog. He's saying, "Please don't kill me, I am so cute!"

If the dog is frightened and growls, lunges, or barks, *do not* verbally or physically reprimand her. Why? By punishing her, she'll make the association that when people are around, bad things happen. Do this enough and she will become a fearful, aggressive dog that will bite people in the future. The way to handle this type of fear display is exactly the same as in the preceding example.

POOCH POINTERS

Gentle stroking calms a dog; vigorous petting energizes a dog. You want calm behaviors here, so gentle is the way to go.

Keep your sessions short—just a few minutes each time. Go to as many different locations as you can, as often as you can, and do the same exercise, rewarding heavily for calm, focused attention on you.

First Contact

When your dog is comfortable just watching people, then you can invite some strangers to come up and pet him. My favorite way is to feed my dog treats while the stranger is petting. That way, positive associations are happening while strangers approach (there's Pavlov again!). If John Q. Public starts to stress your dog out, you can just lure him away with a treat at the earliest signs of stress. If you've done your homework, your dog won't be nervous when strangers lean over him.

An owner feeding a dog while a stranger approaches.
(Photo by P. Dennison)

Please don't skimp or try to rush ahead with these exercises. Your patience will be rewarded. Properly desensitizing your puppy to all sorts of handling takes a little effort in the beginning, but it will pay off in the end. Do your job right and you won't have a dog who needs to be sedated for grooming or toenail clipping.

When introducing your dog to "stuff," be sure to do it gradually. After all, drainpipes can be scary! The best way to handle introductions is to be passive and ignore all but calm reactions to things. If the dog is terrified of a piece of paper, don't laugh, don't comfort, and don't scold. Just stand there quietly—you can laugh hysterically later—and then reinforce calm behavior.

Go through your list of "things my dog needs to get used to" systematically and carefully, and you will have a nice, well-grounded puppy who grows up into a nice, well-adjusted adult.

Pop Quiz

1. What are the typical ages that dogs go through fear periods?

2. While your dog is in a fear period, what is the best thing to do—socialize her more or keep her relatively isolated in familiar and comfortable situations?

3. Does your dog readily accept handling and grooming?

4. How does your dog react around food or bones?

5. Does your dog accept petting willingly or does he avoid your hand as it reaches out?

The Least You Need to Know

- Socialization is a controlled introduction to various situations and things so that the dog develops positive associations with them.

- Work on the basics from the day you get your pup: petting, handling, people food, and food bowls.

- Be sure to watch for any signs of stress. If you spot them, stop training and rethink your next session.
- One puppy kindergarten does not make a well-socialized dog—continue training!

Positive Training in Action

Okay, on to some more training! Let's continue to work on "come," "sit," "down," loose-leash walking, and all the other things that drive us as dog owners crazy. I've broken down the training for each of these behaviors (and more) into tiny steps for you to follow. Go slowly and patiently and refer to this book while you're actually training. You'll be amazed at how quickly your dog will catch on!

You will learn how to utilize reinforcers other than food, how to make things fun and exciting for your dog (and you), and how to properly and positively handle your dog's mistakes.

The Basics Plus Etiquette

In This Chapter

- Please be seated
- Take a load off and lie down
- Proper door protocol
- Settle down!

Sitting, lying down, and standing on cue are extremely useful behaviors. You can use them as alternative behaviors to jumping, for proper greeting behaviors, and for veterinarian visits. They are also the basis for many other behaviors. There's very little your dog can do wrong when he's sitting or lying down.

The great thing is that they're all easy to teach. This chapter also discusses how to teach your dog to behave when he's near an open door.

Puppy Pushups: "Sit," "Down," and "Stand"

The key to teaching the basic behaviors in this section is to associate the correct word with the behavior you want. Your dog is running around the yard and you tell him, "Come." He doesn't know the meaning of the word, but you keep calling him anyway. He is running around, playing with a toy, urinating, barking, and digging, while you scream, "Come!" The next time you say, "Come," he will say to you, "I know what that means!" and run around, play with a toy, urinate, bark, and dig. Why? Because those were the behaviors you paired with the word "come."

> **CANINE CAVEATS**
>
> When teaching any behavior, it's vital that you don't say the word before the behavior happens. You have to add the word for the behavior at precisely the correct time. If you say the word "sit" while the dog is standing, then what behavior have you named "sit"? The "stand"!

"Sit"

Get rid of the old "pull up on the leash and push down on the hind end" method of teaching "sit."

1. Put a treat in your hand and hold your hand up over the dog's head (canine physics in action here—head goes up, butt goes down!). I recommend having your palm facing up for this signal.

2. Do *not* say, "Sit," before the dog sits.

3. When her hind end hits the floor, say, "Sit."

4. Then click and treat.

5. If the dog jumps up, simply take your hand away and try again, perhaps lowering your signal hand.

6. Repeat a few times with a treat in your hand.

7. Then take the treat out of your hand and continue to give your new hand signal (palm up).

8. For now, until the dog learns the behavior, continue to say the word "sit" as the dog's hind end hits the ground.

CANINE CAVEATS

When you start to say the word before the behavior, be sure to say it only once. Don't say, "Sit," repeatedly in the hope that the dog might finally understand. Saying the cue word repeatedly will only teach the dog to respond after the fiftieth "sit."

Say your signal word and then wait for at least 10 seconds. You can say it one more time and wait again for 10 full seconds. If the dog still doesn't respond, go back to using the hand signal a few more times.

A dog sitting.
(Photo by P. Dennison)

It's important to get the food out of your signal hand as soon as possible, because otherwise the dog is just following the treat. Usually you can start saying the word before the behavior after about a week or two. And by that time you can just randomly reinforce the sit—you won't need to treat for each and every one.

"Down"

Now you can teach "down" in the same noninvasive way. You won't have to push down on your dog's shoulders or yank her down by the collar. This would only stress her out anyway, or at the very least, make her more resistant to lying down because you're activating her *opposition reflex*. Here's what to do:

1. Have a treat in your hand.

2. Ask the dog to sit.

3. Bring your hand (slowly) straight down to the ground.

4. When the dog lies down (not before), say, "Down"; then click and treat.

5. Repeat a few times until the dog is lying down faster, and then take the food out of your signal hand, as you did with the "sit."

MUTTLEY MEANINGS

Opposition reflex is the natural reflexive action that makes a dog push or pull against anything that is pushing or pulling against him.

If your dog doesn't lie down right away, make the steps smaller and use tiny approximations. Try this at first on a slippery floor rather than on carpeting.

1. When your dog lowers her head to follow your hand, click and treat.

2. When she lowers her head more, click and treat.

3. After a few repetitions, start to watch her shoulders. Hold your hand steady on the floor. As her shoulders start to lower, click and treat.

4. Continue in this vein and then click and treat when both shoulders are lowered.

5. Usually by this point, on the next try, your dog will lie down. Be sure to click and jackpot with lots of treats.

A dog sitting and his owner starting to lure him into a "down."
(Photo by P. Dennison)

You should see the lightbulb come on in your dog's eyes after a few more repetitions and she'll start to lie down faster and faster.

If your dog won't lie down using this method, don't think that you have a stupid dog; she just doesn't understand what you want. You can try this:

1. Sit on the ground with your leg up, forming a "tent" with your knee. (If your dog is too big to go under your knee, you can use a chair or table rather than your knee.)

2. Have some treats in both hands.

3. Lure the dog under your knee.

4. Do *not* push the dog down with your leg.

5. When the dog's shoulder is under your leg, slowly raise your hand with the treat so that her head follows. Usually she'll lie down at this point.

6. Be sure to say, "Down," and then click and treat.

Repeat a bunch of times until the dog lies down fairly quickly. Now you'll have to fade out your knee:

1. Sit on the floor and don't raise your knee.

2. Move your hand in the same motion, as if you're luring your dog under your leg, but lure next to your leg.

3. When your dog lies down, say, "Down," and click and treat.

After the dog is lying down with a minimum lure from you, you can go back to the earlier steps and lure from a "sit."

I'm sure you've been bending over or kneeling on the ground, so now is the time to start changing your cue to just a hand signal. Otherwise, you'll have to bend over for the rest of the dog's life. Here's what to do:

1. Ask the dog to sit.

2. Stand up straight and bring your signal hand down to the ground. Hold it there until the dog lies down. Then click and treat.

3. Repeat, but this time, bring your hand down to only about two inches off the ground and hold it there. Your dog will probably look at you in confusion, but hold your position. She may also mug your hand. Just stay still. She will lie down. Click and treat when she does.

4. The next step is to bend over so that your hand is now about four inches from the ground. Wait again until your dog lies down. Click and treat when she does.

5. Continue in this vein until you're standing straight and just doing a simple hand motion without bending over. Be sure to stand up straighter, only about two inches at a time.

A handler standing straight up, using a hand signal to tell the dog to go down.
(Photo by P. Dennison)

Do these steps over a few days. Don't forget: too much drilling can be seen as a form of punishment by the dog.

As with the "sit," be sure to continue to say the word "down" as the dog is lying down, not before. It usually takes about two weeks for the dog to learn the behavior reliably. At that time you can then start to say the word "down" before the behavior and as with the sit, go to a random reinforcement schedule when the dog truly understands it.

When practicing the "sits" and "downs," try not to always do them in the same order. Dogs notice patterns. You may think the dog knows the behavior, but she doesn't—she only knows the order in which the behaviors are performed. If you always ask for a "sit" and then a "down," and now you ask for a "down" from a "stand," your dog may look at you blankly. You don't have a stupid dog, you just pattern-trained her. So mix it up and keep her guessing and interested.

CANINE CAVEATS

You may start to notice that your dog responds better to your hand signals than to your verbal signals. Your dog isn't stupid. Dogs are more in tune with their physical environment, which includes your body language. Learning what your spoken words mean is harder for them to figure out than what your hand signals mean.

"Stand"

Stand is useful for grooming, nail clipping, and vet visits. And if you want to compete with your dog at shows, "stand" is a must. Here's how to teach him:

1. Have your dog in a "sit" position on your left side.

2. Put your right hand in front of the dog's nose and slowly lure him, with a treat in your flat hand, into the standing position.

3. Do not say, "Stand," until he does the behavior. As soon as he stands, say, "Stand," and then click and treat.

After a few repetitions, get the treat out of your hand. Be sure to continue to keep your hand flat. Don't forget: dogs watch body language, and a curled hand looks different from a flat hand.

After a few days, you should be able to give the hand signal and say the word "stand" before the behavior. As with the "sit" and "down," don't repeat it a second time. You can just hold your position and wait for the dog to think. If after 10 full seconds he doesn't stand, then just start over with the earlier steps for a day or two.

Holding the treat properly when luring into the "stand."
(Photo by P. Dennison)

Dog is now standing.
(Photo by P. Dennison)

You can start to add petting into the "stand" in preparation for handling and grooming. Begin with a gentle touch, and gradually add real petting.

Miss Manners Would Be Proud: Door Etiquette

Let's say your dog won't sit quietly at the door and charges through each time you open it. You let him do this. Winter comes, your stoop is a sheet of ice, your dog pulls you through the door, and you fall down and hurt your back. Should you be angry at your dog? Nope! *You* trained your dog to charge through the door in the first place!

So what should you do? The obvious solution is to teach "proper door etiquette," or, "Wait at the door until I release you to go through." Follow these steps for the house and the car doors:

1. Approach a door with the dog.

2. Tell the dog "Sit" or "Down." (Be sure to train this before working in the door context.)

3. Put your hand on the doorknob.

4. If the dog stays in position, reinforce the dog.

5. If he moves, ask him to sit again and don't take your hand off the doorknob.

6. Repeat until the dog stays in position.

7. Then turn the knob without opening the door.

8. If the dog stays in position, reinforce the dog. If he moves, ask him to sit again and don't take your hand off the doorknob.

9. Repeat until the dog stays in position.

10. Now it's time to actually open the door a tiny bit. If he moves, ask him to sit, or you can say, "Sit," while you open the door. Reinforce the dog if he doesn't move.

Continue in this manner, opening the door more and more while continuing to reinforce the "sit" and "stay" behavior.

When you can successfully go through the door, you're halfway there! Now it's time to reinforce the dog for looking back to you when you're both through the doorway. This will come in handy when there are distractions on the other side of the door. Do it this way:

1. When you're through the door, say your dog's name.

2. When he looks back, ask for a sit and reinforce him for looking back.

3. Repeat until the dog automatically looks back to you when going through a door without a verbal reminder from you.

Proper door etiquette coming out of the house and car door.
(Photo by P. Dennison)

The dog should learn to automatically look back at you after going through doors.
(Photo by P. Dennison)

I'm Not Dead—My Tail Is Still Wagging: "Settle" and "Roll Over"

"Settle" means to have the dog lie down on his side and stay there. You may also call it "Dead Dog," "Rest," or "Flat." "Roll Over" is obvious—the dog rolls over. Both of these behaviors are useful in handling, grooming, and vet visits.

Luring the dog into a "settle."
(Photo by P. Dennison)

"Settle"

"Settle" is a great behavior for the dog to learn. The uses are many: veterinarian visits, calming behaviors, tick and flea patrol, or any type of physical exam you may need to do. Here's how to teach your dog:

1. Have the dog in a "down."

2. Place your hand with a treat in front of the dog's nose.

3. Lure his head around slowly so that his nose is now facing his rear end.

4. When his elbow collapses under him, move the treat slowly around so that his head is flat on the ground. Click and treat.

5. If the dog gets up, don't worry; just try again.

Right now your hand cue is a big circle, but you can quickly change it to just a small circle with your hand or finger. To get the "stay" part of this exercise, use your pointer finger touching the ground as a helper cue, and then feed the treats from that hand. Fade out the treats in that hand as quickly as possible. It usually takes only a few days.

When the dog is comfortable with the "settle," you can add gentle petting or an exam of genital areas and feet, always clicking and treating the dog for not moving. If the dog moves away, just try again—perhaps you went too fast or were petting in a place that he's uncomfortable with.

You can also be very creative when adding a cue word for this and other trick behaviors. Think about it ahead of time so that you can add the cue word or hand motion from the beginning. My absolute favorite line is, "I am going to hypnotize you. When I count to three and snap my fingers, you will fall asleep. One, two, three (snap)." The snapping of your fingers is the cue for the dog to settle.

Adding the examination during the "settle."
(Photo by P. Dennison)

"Roll Over"

"Roll over" is the obvious next step after teaching the "settle." "Roll over" is a great behavior to teach because it gets the dog acclimated to someone leaning over her. Here's what to do:

1. When your dog is in the "down" position, use the same luring movement that you started with doing the "settle."

2. Now, instead of luring your dog's head to lie flat on the ground, continue to lure so that she rolls over completely. This may mean (depending on the size of dog you have) that you'll have to lean over her.

3. As soon as she rolls over, click and treat.

Luring the dog from a "settle" into a "roll over."
(Photo by P. Dennison)

If she doesn't roll over right away or is nervous about your leaning over her, be sure to break down the steps into smaller ones. At each step of her head moving in the correct direction, click and treat. Be sure to move your hand slowly, and try not to get too excited about her getting it instantly. Small steps in easy training sessions will keep her interested in the game.

Pop Quiz

1. What is opposition reflex?

2. How many "sits" or "downs" (or other good behaviors) does your dog do before you reward him?

3. Why is it *not* a good idea to ask for the same behaviors in exactly the same order?

The Least You Need to Know

- "Sits," "downs," and "stands" are more important than you think.
- Training proper door etiquette can save both you and your dog some injuries.
- Hands-off training will get you there faster.
- Settling and rolling over come in handy in many situations.

Loose-Leash Walking

Chapter 10

In This Chapter

- Why do dogs pull? To get to the other side!
- Being more interesting than your environment
- Leash-walking exercises and games
- Using sniffing to your advantage

Loose-leash walking is such an important topic, and one that most people can relate to, that I've devoted this entire chapter to it. I've known some fantastic dogs who have been dumped in shelters just because they pull on the leash. There are many nuances to walking on a loose leash; this is not just a simple behavior.

Why Dogs Pull

You want to peacefully walk your dog, but your dog suddenly picks up a scent and takes off at warp speed. Your walks have become a nightmare and you almost wish you could undo his housetraining because cleaning up messes on the carpet would be easier than walking him.

A dog taking his owner for a walk.
(Photo by P. Dennison)

You sweat, curse, scream, yank back—in desperation you use a choke or prong collar. Finally, you declare your dog stupid, stubborn, disobedient, or even dominant. What has actually happened is that you've systematically trained your dog to pull on the leash. Congratulations! You learned how to activate his opposition reflex, and you taught him that to get where he wants to go, he has to pull you down the street.

Dogs do not pull "because they can," and they truly haven't been up all night, scheming in their devious doggie minds how to annoy you to death by giving you whiplash. There are very specific reasons why dogs pull on the leash that don't involve dislocating your shoulder.

Because We Follow

The number one reason why dogs pull on the leash is this: because we follow. Behavior is reward driven. If choking himself gets him what he wants—to move forward in any direction he so chooses—then guess what? He'll continue to pull.

Pulling on the leash then becomes a learned behavior, and a very strong one at that. "Fanatical" and "overzealous" are words that can be used to describe many dogs' leash-wrenching techniques, as they practice it to perfection.

Of course, they want to make us happy. "You like it when I pull a little, so you should like it even better when I pull a lot." So what starts out as a little pulling can quickly become a "run for your money, might as well wear roller blades" event because "more is better," right?

To Get to the Other Side

The number two reason why dogs pull on the leash is to get to the other side. There are actually two parts to this. First, the outside world is an exciting and wonderfully smelly place for a dog. It is a veritable smorgasbord of scent.

> **DOGGIE DATA**
>
> Did you know that a dog has 20 to 40 times more olfactory receptors than a human? Some dogs can find bodies, dead or alive, by following scents of shed skin flakes, sweat droplets, and scent mists for as long as 105 hours and as far as 135 miles. Many dogs can also "fore-smell" seizures in humans and detect skin-cancer cells.

Scent is extremely important to a dog—after all, they're predators. Yes, even a Maltese or Miniature Poodle. Dogs process a great deal of information about their world through their noses. We've all seen our dogs sniff one single blade of grass for 15 minutes and think that it is a bit excessive. However, it's not without meaning for a dog. He finds out who was there and when, who is in season, and how many bitches and how many males have been there.

Second, the dog forgets that we exist. We are no more important than a speck of dust. There are many reasons for this seeming lack of respect. Most people train their dogs in the living room and never take it on the road. They're shocked and dismayed that their dog blows them off when outside.

The biggest challenge we all come up against is to be more interesting and reinforcing to our dogs than the environment. Whether you're doing pet training or competition training, whether you're a first-time dog owner or an accomplished dog trainer, being more compelling than the environment is always a challenge.

That challenge can be drudgery or it can be fun, enlightening, and immensely rewarding if you have the right attitude. The key here is one of the basics of positive dog training: the relationship between you and your dog. There are many facets to building a bond with your dog. Associative learning—making sure fun things happen around you at all times—tops the chart. Also up there are having patience at all times, training in manners, and being variable and unpredictable in when and how you reinforce your dog.

Opposition Reflex

The number three reason why dogs pull on the leash is this: because we activate their opposition reflex, which causes them to pull against anything that's pulling against them.

Try this test. Have someone stand next to you. Push on that person's arm. If that person doesn't want to fall, that person will push back so that he or she isn't knocked over. Now pull on the person's arm. If the person doesn't want to be yanked toward you, he or she will pull back.

Building an Outdoor Relationship

Okay, now that you know why everything you've tried so far to stop your dog from pulling on the leash hasn't worked, let's move on to what does work.

The first step to loose-leash walking is building your relationship outdoors. This isn't hard, but it does take some forethought. You have to teach your dog that there's no such thing as a free lunch. After all, you have to work for a living, and the dogs should, too.

Attention, Please!

Before teaching any behavior outdoors, you must build your relationship and get the dog's attention. If you hand-feed your dog most of her intake of food for behaviors, rather than give it to her for "free" in her bowl, her wish is your command:

1. Take your dog's daily ration of food, mix in some smelly treats, put it in your pockets or pouch, and go outside.

2. Work on eye contact, name recognition, "sits" and "downs," and anything else your dog may know how to do at the moment. (For more details, see Chapters 7 and 9.)

3. If your dog is too stimulated by your yard, just wait. Whenever she gives you some kind of attention, reward it.

4. If, after about 10 minutes, she still hasn't noticed that you exist, put her back in the house and in her crate for a few minutes and try again later.

POOCH POINTERS

If the dog doesn't notice that you exist, ask yourself questions such as, "Are the distractions too much for my dog to handle at this time in his training?" "Did I go from the living room to the football game in one step?" "Was I distracted or not in the mood?" Always set the dog up to succeed and he will!

Continue to do this for a few days—feeding for attention and simple behaviors. Now move to a new location and start all over, waiting patiently for attention and simple behaviors. Every few days, move to a new location and repeat all of the preceding steps.

You must establish this very simple foundation—getting and keeping your dog's attention—before moving on to the next step. Try loose-leash walking without it and you'll get tight-leash pulling. The dog has to know that you aren't a dead tree stump. After about one to two weeks of practicing in about five to seven spots, you'll be ready to start training for loose-leash walking.

Play Is the First Step

I like teaching a "heel" first and then a loose-leash "walk." That way, your dog will develop a history of paying attention to you, which makes loose-leash walking a cinch! Dogs think about what they're looking at, so if they aren't looking at you, they aren't thinking about you, either. "Heel" is when your dog is on your left side, his head by the seam of your pants as he looks up at you adoringly.

To start out teaching a "heel," play is your first step. Why? Because heeling is a team sport and it is important that your dog learns to pay attention to you while you are both moving. With the two of you facing each other, just feint left and right in a very excited manner and click and treat your dog for following you. Be very enthusiastic; otherwise he may not follow you. Practice this in a few locations for a few days.

Moving Backups

Your second step to teaching "heel" is moving backups:

1. After playing for a minute or so, take a few steps backward. Click and treat if the dog follows you. You're not looking for eye contact yet—you just want him to follow you. Be sure to back up in weavy lines—straight is boring for most dogs.

2. Don't lure your dog with cookies—have your hands down by your sides. If he mugs your hands, put them behind your back.

3. Take a few more steps back and click and treat every few steps.

4. Gradually increase the number of steps you back up before clicking and treating. Now you can wait for eye contact before you click and treat. Mix and match between playing and backing up.

A dog and his handler doing moving backups.
(Photo by P. Dennison)

Some dogs are successful with this game within a few minutes and some dogs take hours to stay around their owners. If your dog is one of the few who won't focus on you, please don't be angry. Just backtrack and work on more focus at home first. If your dog looks away, you can either continue to back up and click and treat when he comes back into position, or stop moving and wait for the dog to reengage with you (by giving you eye contact); then continue to back up and then click and treat.

DOGGIE DATA

When I switched over from traditional training to positive training, playing the long-line game was great practice for me to get rid of my old habit of popping and jerking my dog's leash. You can't pop and jerk if you aren't holding a leash. In addition, it really forced me to build my relationship, rather than to rely on a leash to keep my dog with me.

Pivot to Heel

After your dog is following you, put the leash and clicker in your *right* hand and the treats in your left hand. When he is really looking at you, pivot to your right, so the dog is now on your left. Click and treat with your left hand.

After each click and treat, place your left hand up at your tummy. This will become your heel cue—bent left arm. Take a few steps forward and click and treat again. Use a high rate of reinforcement at first and gradually use less and less food for more and more heeling.

Why feed with your left hand? Because if your dog is on the left and you feed with your right hand, he will cross in front of you and trip you!

Don't name this yet, because if you name a sub-standard behavior, that's what you'll get when you ask for it. Wait until it is as perfect as you want it to be and then name it. While in training mode, I use an interim word, such as "let's go." When you like what you see, you can start to name it your real cue. "Heel," "strut," "with me," and "march" are the most common heel cue words.

Heeling Games

Start to make heeling fun, by adding in turns and halts with automatic sits. As you are about to turn to the right (away from your dog), pause for an instant, say his name and "this way." When he stays up to you as you turn, click and treat.

To teach an automatic sit, simply lure your dog into a "sit" (and verbally say, "Sit") as you are about to stop. Do this a dozen or so times and your dog will automatically sit when you stop.

There may come a time when you are presented with something you don't want your dog to engage with—such as a skunk, bear, deer, aggressive dog, cat, whatever. You need your dog's attention and you need it *fast!* Practice this in advance and you'll have that instant response when you need it.

As you are heeling, just back up a few steps as you call your dog to come and have him sit in front of you. Click and treat. You can also practice grabbing his collar (see Chapter 8) in case you get boxed in somewhere.

Playing Follow the Leader

My favorite way to teach heeling is to actually start without a leash. If your dog wants to stay with you without a leash, then adding the leash is a piece of cake. To start this, I like to play "follow the leader" with the dog on a 50-foot line or off-leash completely in a safe, fenced-in area.

Arm yourself with wads of yummy treats and follow these steps:

1. Give your dog one treat.

2. Walk away. Don't use any verbal cues or commands with this game. You want your dog to stay with you because she *wants* to, not because you're forcing her to do so with the leash, or constantly prodding her verbally.

3. If your dog follows you, feed her treats and pet and praise her for a full 20 seconds.

4. Now change direction. If your dog stays with you, reinforce her again for a full 20 seconds. After each reinforcer, change direction.

5. Repeat until your dog stays by your side as you move around.

6. If your dog comes toward you but charges on ahead, turn around and walk away from her. This is where you don't want to look at her butt. The name of this game is "follow the leader," and she isn't the leader, you are.

7. Keep repeating until your dog stays with you.

Loose-Leash Walking

When your dog is successfully heeling, either on- or off-leash, you can start training a loose-leash walk. My definition of loose-leash walking is that the dog can be anywhere—in front, on the right or left, or even behind, as long as the leash is loose. Above all, remember, the leash is *not* a tool. It is a safety net!

POOCH POINTERS

If you've taught your dog to pull on a collar, you may want to consider switching to a harness. My two favorite types of harnesses are listed in Appendix B.

Try to start this in a low-distraction area. As always, you want to set the dog up for success as much as possible. After all, I bet you didn't learn to drive on a major highway—you probably started in an empty parking lot. Gradually work up to heavy distractions. The higher the distraction level, the higher value your reinforcers should be.

Take your dog out for a walk, preferably on at least a 15-foot leash. (Don't use a retractable lead—they actually encourage dogs to pull because there is always tension on the dog's neck.) Your left arm will be straight down, which signals a loose-leash walk (if your left arm is bent, that is your nonverbal heel cue). Click for the leash being loose and then just toss the dog a treat. If you feed in heel position, your dog will go back to heeling. Not a bad thing really, but we're now teaching a loose-leash walk. I have found that when the owner is concentrating on their dog, they lose sight of whether the lead is loose. By using a longer leash, you'll have more time to react and get that click and treat in before the leash gets taut.

It's really that simple. I taught my Border Collie, Emma (who I think was a sled dog in a previous life), to loose-leash walk this way after nothing, and I mean nothing, stopped her from pulling. Her heeling was perfect, but loose-leash walking—nope. All it took was two 15-minute sessions and the lightbulb went on in her furry brain.

Practice going from heel to loose-leash walk to heel and back again. Make it fun!

Does "be a tree" really work? Maybe. I say maybe because if you do it right (just as with anything else), it works. Do it wrong and it goes south pretty quickly. "Be a tree" is not my favorite method for teaching loose-leash walking, but some people find it effective.

The wrong way: You stop moving when your dog pulls and then reward him right away when he stops pulling. This will only teach him to pull, stop, get a treat. Cha-cha-cha.

The right way: You stop moving when your dog pulls, move forward again, and *then* reward him for walking nicely. You can change direction while he is looking toward you (so as not to jerk his collar), and/or pat your leg to encourage him to stay with you—long enough to reinforce the correct loose-leash walking behavior.

Your Worst Distraction Can Be Your Greatest Ally

I can hear you groaning already! Dogs, kids, leaves, planes, cars, bicycles, deer, squirrels, birds, smells of all kinds, cats—the list is endless and frustrating. How can you use these distractions to your benefit? Build a strong positive relationship with your dog, and become your dog's benevolent "Higher Power."

You've laid the groundwork by hand-feeding your dog for behaviors for a few weeks and now you have her attention outside. You've been practicing "follow the leader," "heel," and some loose-leash walking in a relatively distraction-free area. You're doing a great job!

After you've built a solid foundation, you can use the distractions that have driven you crazy to help build your relationship to an even higher level. Use her sniffing as a reward for walking nicely by your side. Follow these steps:

1. Get a few steps of loose-leash walking (perhaps starting on a parking lot—let's make it easy for the dog to succeed).

2. Then run over to some grass and while you point to the ground, say, "Go sniff."

3. Let her have a penny's worth of sniffing and then verbally encourage her, without using the leash to drag her (or lure her with food or toys if you have to the first few times), to come back to you.

4. Heavily reward her recall, even if at first it wasn't all that prompt.

5. Do a few more steps of loose-leash walking and reward again with some sniffing.

Within a few repetitions, you should see your dog start to sniff less and less, and to be interested in you for longer periods of time. Why should this be so? Because you've ceased to be a barrier to her fun and are now her active partner.

Pop Quiz

1. If you stop moving when your dog starts to pull, should you reinforce him the instant he comes back to you?

2. If you let your dog pull on-leash sometimes and not other times, what is your dog learning?

3. If you yank on the leash when he is pulling, what is your dog learning?

4. Have you started to use other types of reinforcers for loose-leash walking? Have you noticed a positive difference in his attention to you?

The Least You Need to Know

- Dogs pull because we follow, because they want to smell things, and because of the opposition reflex.
- Build your outdoor relationship first before teaching loose-leash walking.

- After you've decided to teach loose-leash walking, never let the dog pull again.
- Stop being a barrier to your dog's fun; use what she wants as a reward for walking nicely.

Teaching the "Stays"

In This Chapter

- Learning to stay one second at a time
- Learning the three "D"s: distance, duration, and distraction
- Teaching how to "Wait right there!"
- Teaching your dog that patience is rewarded

The "stays" are almost as hard to teach as loose-leash walking. We spend much of our time training our dogs to stay close to us and heavily rewarding them for it. Now we want them to stay way over there. Can't we humans make up our minds?

"Stays" are difficult to teach but very important, and can be life-saving for our dogs. They are helpful when you have a multiple-dog household to stop them from getting in your way and tripping you while you're running for the phone.

"Stays" are useful for the vet's office, grooming, toenail clipping, or waiting at the front door, car door, and crate door before you release them. They're essential for competition obedience, agility, sheep herding, and any other dog sport.

In addition, "stays" are great for teaching your dog to stay on his mat, so that you can eat dinner without being mauled or without the dog begging (although all begging behavior is caused by someone feeding the dog from the table, thus reinforcing the dog for begging).

"Sit," "Down," and "Stand Stay"

Obviously, to start teaching the "stays," you must already have trained the "sit," "down," and "stand" behaviors. Please review Chapter 9 before attempting "stays."

An easy way to teach "stays" is simply this (and for this behavior alone, I don't use the clicker):

1. Ask your dog to sit.

2. Remind him to "sit," pivot your upper torso away (keep your feet planted), and go right back in and treat.

3. Repeat step 2 until your dog is solid.

4. Remind him to "sit" again and this time, start to take a step, but keep one foot planted. Go back in and treat.

5. When he is staying nicely, turn away and one step at a time leave him.

You'll notice that I am not asking you to say "stay" yet. Wait until it is perfect; for now, just use a reminder cue of "sit." At any time if he breaks the "stay," just go back and reposition him and try again. When you are approximately 10 to 15 feet away and he hasn't budged, then you can start adding the word "stay." I use "sit stay" as a transition and then eventually get rid of the "sit" part. For the "down" as well as the "stand," you'll do the same steps as previously listed.

Be sure you turn your back to the dog when you leave. Backing away while chanting, "Stay, stay, stay," won't work in the long run and won't work in real life. You'll need to turn away from him to deal and if you don't practice that, then he'll break his stay and possibly get hurt.

POOCH POINTERS

If you ask your dog to "sit," and she sits and then goes into a "down," this does not constitute a "stay." "Stay" means, "Stay in that position until I come back and release you."

If your dog breaks at any point, you must ignore him for about 15 seconds and then just reset the session. Make sure the dog won't run out in traffic when you ignore him. Be prudent. Be safe. When you add each new distraction, you must start again at level one.

Adding Distractions

Next up—the dreaded distractions! The list is endless. Kids, bikes, cars, dogs, people, birds, squirrels, deer—you name it, it can be a distraction.

Start out with mild distractions—say, one other person walking slowly around. Then have the person walk faster, then jog, then run. Then add another person, and another. You can start to add toys (not teasing the dog) and other types of distractions. Always be sure that you add them slowly, and always set the dog up for success.

POOCH POINTERS

If you've done your homework, building your relationship and recalls amidst distractions, this shouldn't be too hard.

Be sure that, after you start a higher intensity of distractions, you go back to level one of the time chart. If the dog breaks, say to yourself, "No big deal," and just try again. Please stay away from any verbal "corrections." Silence works best.

Wait a Minute!

Many people use just one word—"*stay*"—to mean a few different things. I like using two words: "*stay*" and "*wait*." To me, they have different meanings. "Stay" means, "You stay there until I come back to you." "Wait" means, "Wait there until I give you another cue." If you feel more comfortable using just one word, that's not a problem as long as you're clear in your direction. Do what you'll remember and what you'll be consistent with.

Two important uses of the "stay"/"wait" are to have the dog go to her mat and "stay" there, and to "wait" for dinner.

Go to Your Mat!

Let's teach your dog to go to his mat. You may not think this is any big deal and that your dog doesn't need to know this, but it can be a useful behavior.

If your dog is bugging you and you're busy, you can tell him to go to his "mat," "bed," or "place"—whatever word you want to use. For dogs who have been reinforced for begging at the table, this is great. Basically, this is "target training." You're teaching your dog to "target" the mat and lie down on it and stay there. Follow these steps:

1. Have a mat or bed set up.

2. Sit in a chair about five feet away.

3. Throw cookies onto the mat and don't say anything yet.

4. As the dog steps on the mat, click and throw some more treats.

5. Repeat this about 24 times.

6. If the dog goes back to the mat of his own accord, click and throw treats. (We're now getting the behavior, and then rewarding, rather than luring the dog onto the mat with the treats.)

At this point you still won't say anything to the dog. Get the full behavior, and *then* give it a name. Dogs aren't really listening to us, anyway, and do better if we're quiet and let them think.

Now stop throwing cookies onto the mat. Look at your dog. After he has also engaged your eye contact, look at the mat. Look at his face again and then look at the mat. If he looks at the mat or goes over to the mat, click and throw the treat on the mat. If he doesn't move, look at him again and then stare at the mat. For any movement toward the mat, be it head or body movement, you should click and throw cookies onto the mat.

Take the tape off of your mouth now—you can start talking! Follow these steps:

1. When your dog goes to the mat either on his own or with the help of your eye, as he steps on the mat, say, "Go to your mat/place/bed" (whatever you want to call it).

2. Then click and treat the behavior.

3. Repeat this about 10 times.

4. Then do a test. When he's off the mat, say, "Go to your mat," and wait—see what he does.

5. If he goes to the mat, click and jackpot. If he doesn't, just backtrack.

6. When your dog goes to the mat on a regular basis, go to him (because you're at least five feet away) and lure him into a "sit" and then a "down." Reward the "down."

I ask you to go to him because if you're any real distance from him, he'll get off the mat and come to you to "sit" and "down." So you need to teach him to work away from you for this exercise, which is why you have to either lean forward or move forward to help him in the beginning.

Very quickly, your dog will, upon hearing you say, "Go to your mat," go to the mat and lie down. Now you have to build distance, duration, and changing *location*.

DOGGIE DATA

My dog Cody taught me (without speaking one word of English) that by staring in the direction I want a dog to look, he'll turn his head that way. After I gave each of my dogs a bone, Cody came up to me after about 10 minutes, whining and turning his head repeatedly. I normally ignore him when he whines because I don't want to reinforce whining. However, I did glance at him out of the corner of my eye and realized he was looking at Beau and then back to me. Beau had stolen Cody's bone and he wanted me to get it back for him. Try it sometime—it is just too cool! And you never know, you may just find a use for it someday.

Changing location is great to work on—move the mat to different parts of the house and yard. Wouldn't it be great to go to a softball game, bring your mat, and ask the dog to go to her mat and she does it! And stays there! And doesn't annoy the other people there! Wow!

You'll also need to build distance. Let's say you're in the kitchen and the mat is in the living room. Your dog wants attention, but you're talking on the phone and cooking dinner and you're transferring hot things from the stove to the table—not a good time for your dog to decide "It's playtime!" That's a perfect time to tell your dog to go to her mat.

When building distance, be sure to move away from the mat only a few feet at a time. Just as when you were teaching "stays," building distance slowly is important to the success of the behavior.

Waiting for Dinner

Waiting for dinner may not seem like a behavior you'll need, but it's an excellent and simple way to introduce the word "*wait*" into your dog's vocabulary. I like it because it teaches self-control to the dog so that she doesn't get pushy and forceful around food.

Follow these steps:

1. Put a few pieces of food in a bowl on the counter.

2. Ask the dog to sit.

3. Start to put the bowl on the floor.

4. If at any time she moves out of position, take the bowl away.

5. Remind the dog to sit again.

6. Repeat steps three and four. Don't add the word "*wait*" yet—again, silence is best. Get the behavior first—then name it. After a few repetitions of steps three and four, you won't even have to remind the dog to sit again—she will most likely fix herself.

7. After the dog waits for even one second, click and release her to the food bowl.

8. As soon as she waits for two seconds, you can say the word *"wait."*

9. You can increase the wait time to be as long as you wish.

This easily transfers to "wait" in the car, in the crate, or at the door, all of which may just save her life one day. "Stays" can be boring to teach, but the benefits are enormous, so please don't skimp on training them.

CANINE CAVEATS

Pushiness around food or toys is not acceptable behavior. Many people misinterpret this behavior as being dominant, when in fact it's just the behavior of an untrained, spoiled dog who was probably reinforced in the past for being obnoxious.

Pop Quiz

1. If you have built up to 30 seconds of a "stay" in your living room, how many seconds should you start at each new location?

2. Have you started to work on "wait" for the food bowl?

3. How far away have you gotten so far from her mat?

The Least You Need to Know

- Take it literally one step at a time and your dog will have a solid "stay."
- Start out building duration with little or no distraction; then add distance to your "stays."
- After you have distance and duration, you can add distractions.
- Practice "go to your mat" and "wait for the food bowl" to build your dog's patience and self-control.

What If Your Dog Makes a Mistake?

Chapter 12

In This Chapter

- If at first you don't succeed, proceed!
- Finally, a *real* reason to clean your house!
- Don't get mad ...
- Necessity is the mother of invention

If your dog makes a mistake, you need to stop and look at the situation. Did you make the mistake—giving wrong or different cues or pushing the dog beyond her limits? Did you train the dog with enough correct repetitions and contexts? Don't blame the dog. If you teach a behavior incorrectly or don't train enough, then it isn't the dog's fault if she responds incorrectly.

Let's look at some different positive options to pursue when your dog makes a mistake. Not everything works for every dog or every situation, but there's always a positive solution if you look for it.

Give Me a "P": Proceed, Putting It on Cue

Two easy strategies for dealing with an incorrect response are to proceed and to put it on cue. These methods are great because they give you the chance to regroup, rethink, and go scream in the closet if you're getting angry. They also give you the opportunity to be creative in stopping some behaviors that are less than wonderful.

Proceed: Moving On to Something Else

After three tries, if your dog just isn't getting it today, instead of repeating the routine again and again (which can be seen as a punishment because the dog is not being reinforced for the mistakes), move on to something else or give both of you a breather.

This also gives you the opportunity to rethink your training strategy. It's very important to know exactly how to teach each behavior before you even take the dog out for training. Trainers at SeaWorld and most of the positive dog trainers I know do this. They all get together and discuss in detail what each session will entail:

- What behavior they will work on
- What approximation of that behavior they will accept
- How many repetitions they will do
- What they will do if the animal doesn't respond correctly
- What the reinforcers will be
- How many minutes each session will last
- How many minutes of downtime there will be between each session
- How many total sessions they will have per day

Putting It on Cue

This means to cue and reinforce the bad behavior you don't like so that the dog learns to perform the bad behavior only on cue. Then don't ever give the cue!

I did this with Beau, one of my Border Collies. On rainy days I have towels by the back door to wipe the dogs' feet as they come in from the backyard mud field. Well, Beau thought that was really cool and would steal the towels and start to shred them.

So I put the towel-stealing behavior on cue. I call it "mop the floor" (because he likes to shake the towel, pretending that he's killing it).

In the beginning, I would say, "Mop the floor" for stealing a towel and then click and treat him. I did this dozens of times, and now on rainy days he will not take a towel unless I say, "Mop the floor."

As they say, "If you can't beat 'em, join 'em." In the dog-training world, we say, "Put it under *stimulus control* and never give the cue!"

MUTTLEY MEANINGS

Stimulus control means that the dog responds promptly to a cue in any and all situations. Some people say that barking can be put under stimulus control, but I've never seen it work. Barking seems to be an incredibly self-reinforcing behavior for some dogs, and they'll do it anyway, cued or not.

Give Me an "A": Administration, Aid, Antecedent

Setting the dog up to be right is key here. It's counterproductive, not to mention silly, to set the dog up to fail and then get angry at him for failing.

Being frustrated is normal, and taking it out on the dog is easy. Your dog doesn't speak English and sometimes that makes training hard. However, there are easy answers.

Administration or Management

If your dog eats your shoes, put them away! If your dog gets into the garbage can, find one with a locking lid. If you know a certain stimulus upsets or overexcites your dog, use better judgment in introducing the stimulus to your dog. Then work on desensitizing your dog to it.

Don't wait for something bad to happen—stop the behavior before it starts. Practicing bad behaviors does no one any good. Plus, it might make you angry and you may do something that you'll regret in the morning. After all, you would baby-proof a house, and you should doggie-proof it as well.

Aid

Give the dog an easier version of the behavior you're working on that she can solve successfully: shorten the time, distance, duration, or complexity.

For instance, let's say you're teaching your dog to "stay," and you've built up to one minute in an area that has no distractions. Good job! Now you go to the ballgame, which is much more diverting than your empty living room. Don't ask your dog to "stay" for one minute—she won't be successful. Try for three seconds to start, and build up slowly to one minute.

Antecedent

Give the dog some clear, intermediate helper cues so that she can understand more clearly what it is you want. This can be a verbal reminder cue, "Stay," or an additional hand signal. The key is not to do rapid-fire reminder cues—then you get stuck in a rut saying "Sit-sit-sit-sit-sit" and sound like a machine gun. Dogs don't speak English, but they sure can count! Don't confuse them even more when your task is to help them.

In addition, be sure that your cues are consistent and accurate. If sometimes you call your dog to come and you're standing up straight, and sometimes bending over, or sitting, or kneeling, you'll have one very confused doggie. If your cue for "down" is normally a raised hand like a traffic cop but one day you just raise your hand high in the sky, don't be surprised when the dog looks at you blankly.

Give Me an "I": Incompatible, Ignore, Innovation

Now is the time to get a bit inventive. I've given you some of my favorite options to jumpstart your creative juices. Incompatible behaviors will save your sanity, so teach your dog to do all the behaviors in this book—they are all incompatible with fear, aggression, and nervousness. They also give the dog a "job" to do. If you don't give your dog a job, he will become self-employed, and you most likely won't like the career change.

Incompatible

Give your dog a cue (one that he knows well) that's incompatible with the bad behavior he's doing at the moment. For instance, if you tell the dog to sit, that's incompatible with jumping. He can't be jumping if he's sitting. Or, after your dog has excellent name recognition (see Chapter 7), you can say his name to get his attention and then give him a cue to a different behavior to keep him otherwise occupied.

Training incompatible behaviors is one of my favorite ways of solving behavior problems. Sometimes it just takes a bit of thought to come up with a solution.

If your dog goes crazy every time the doorbell rings, train him that the sound of the doorbell means, "Go to your crate." Or let's say that every time your dog sees someone, he wants to fling himself at that person. Teach him that a person approaching is a cue to "sit." Or if you want to allow him to approach a person, teach him to "go visit," meaning to go to the person you're pointing to and lie down—which is incompatible with jumping.

Ignoring the Dog

If the dog is doing something bad, ignore him until he gives you a good behavior that you can then reinforce. For example, if your dog is barking at someone or something, just stand still until he's quiet, wait for 10 seconds, and then reinforce the quiet behavior. By yelling or petting to calm him down, you're actually reinforcing the inappropriate behavior, which you don't want to do. If, after 15 seconds or so, the dog hasn't regained control of himself, move away, redirect onto appropriate behaviors, and then reinforce the dog for good behaviors.

If the dog is ignoring you, leave the area and have him search for you. Let him know that you aren't irrelevant or just a piece of furniture that happens to be at the end of the leash. Use good judgment when walking away from your dog during training. Don't disappear if the area isn't safe and secure for your dog.

DOGGIE DATA

Here's a quiz: Kate had problems with her 14-month-old dog, Chloë. Chloë was constantly jumping and biting for attention, and she'd been doing this since she was 12 weeks old. If she didn't get instant attention, Chloë would become more frantic and bite harder, especially if there was food around.

Question: Why was Chloë doing this, and what can be done to stop it?

Answer: Kate admitted to reinforcing the jumping and mouthing by giving Chloë attention by petting or yelling at her. To fix Chloë's behavior, Kate should ignore her inappropriate behaviors and reward her heavily for not bothering humans and for being calm around food; she could also teach Chloë to do really fast sits. (Sitting is incompatible with jumping and biting.)

Innovation

Try changing your rewards to something new that the dog really craves. No matter how much you like M&M's, there's probably a point at which you've had enough, and the same thing happens to your dog. Use all different types of food, toys, silly games, petting, and praise to reinforce your dog.

Being variable and unpredictable is the key to enriching your dog's life and training. Chapter 14 has a full discussion on the "how" of variable reinforcement.

Give Me an "R": Repeat, Redirect, Recreation, Restrain

Watch and listen to your dog. If you pay attention to what she's telling you, most of the time you can come up with an easy solution. If you have a good relationship with your dog, she really does want to do what you're asking her. If all of a sudden she looks at you blankly, please don't assume that she's stupid.

Repeating the Cue a Second Time

Try one more time by using clearer cues, such as a hand signal. Wait for at least 10 seconds before repeating the command so that the dog learns to perform immediately after the first command. Don't repeat the command a third time! You don't want your command to be "Sit-sit-sit!"

By waiting patiently for at least 10 seconds, you're giving the dog the opportunity to *think!* Remember when you were first learning a foreign language? Did you remember all of those new words the first time out? In addition, please don't forget: humans are a verbal species and dogs are not!

Redirect

Redirect to better behavior. If your dog eats the sofa, learn what she usually does just before eating the sofa—sniffing the floor, running around, barking, or whining—and stop the sofa destruction *before* it happens.

You can distract her with a toy when she just starts to think about eating the sofa, but don't try to play with her *after* she has already started. This will only reinforce the sofa-eating behavior. You can still distract, but then give her at least three other behaviors to do and then reinforce her. Either put the dog in the crate or engage her in some stimulating activity.

Dogs who incessantly bark or chew are usually understimulated, bored, or have been inadvertently reinforced (with your attention or bad timing of reinforcement) for doing the very behavior that's driving you crazy. Remember: Behavior is reward driven!

Be sure to pay plenty of attention to your dog when she's not doing anything bad!

Recreation

Use tiredness to your advantage: a dog who is fully exercised, both mentally and physically, is less likely to bark, chew, jump up, or otherwise drive you insane.

Giving the dog enough vigorous exercise *with you* is excellent preventive therapy! My motto is, "A tired dog is a good dog." A placid walk around the block is not enough aerobic exercise to physically tire out most dogs. Playing fetch, swimming, playing with another dog, jogging, and hiking are all good ways to keep your dog fit and to tire her out. This is the ultimate incompatible behavior: a sleeping dog can do no harm.

> **DOGGIE DATA**
>
> I prefer activities that the two of you can do together. Because classical conditioning (remember Ivan Pavlov?) is always happening, you might as well take advantage of it and pair yourself with all sorts of fun things for your dog. That way, you have a tired dog and a dog that associates good stuff with you. It's a win-win situation.

Restrain

Confine or contain the dog. But be sensible! If imminent danger threatens, get your dog out of there!

If the dog is veering into traffic, or if a loose dog bent on rearranging you or your dog's face is in attack mode, get out of there. Although it's preferable to wait out a bad reaction from your dog so that you can then reinforce good behavior, there are times when a fast retreat is best. If the dog is so incredibly overaroused that she's foaming at the mouth, spit is flying everywhere, and her eyes are glazed, then get her out of there—now!

There's time enough later, when everyone is calm, to assess the situation dispassionately and carefully. If the situation was something out of your control—such as a loose dog with no owner in sight—you can read Chapter 5 on familiarizing yourself with calming signals. Many times you can use these to disarm a dog who is showing aggressive behaviors.

> **DOGGIE DATA**
>
> Patty was out with her dog, Mike, when they came upon a loose dog running around, growling at every dog in his path. There was no way of restraining the loose dog, so Patty quickly and calmly asked Mike to lie down (a calming signal). She kept Mike's attention on her, rather than risk his reacting to the errant dog. The instant Mike lay down, the approaching dog slowed his pace, sniffed Mike in a half-hearted fashion, and then went about his doggie way.

Above all, think about what *you're* doing to encourage your dog to behave in a certain way. If your dog does something you don't like on a regular basis, watch *yourself* to see whether you're inadvertently reinforcing that very behavior!

For instance, if your dog repeatedly steals your clothes and then you chase after him in a merry game of keep-away, your dog thinks "What fun, Mommy! Thanks!" Do you yell at the dog? (Remember—negative attention is still attention.) Now he thinks, "Wow, Mom is turning purple *and* chasing me all over the house! Thanks, Mom!" Before getting angry, think to yourself, "What is the dog finding reinforcing?"

So we now have a P, an A, an I, and an R. What does that spell? *PAIR!* You and your dog are a pair, a team, best friends, a match made in heaven! So let's give the *dog* a B-R-E-A-K!

Pop Quiz

1. Have you started planning your sessions better?

2. Name at least five alternative options you can utilize if your dog makes a mistake.

3. Have you inadvertently reinforced your dog for any bad behaviors?

The Least You Need to Know

- If your dog doesn't respond correctly after three tries, move on to something else.
- Stop bad behaviors before they start; be a helper and set your dog up for success.
- If your dog does something bad, redirect him to an incompatible behavior, such as lying down.
- Get your human emotions out of dog training—they don't belong there!

The Premack Principle

Chapter 13

In This Chapter

* Deciding what you want your dog to do
* Identifying what your dog wants
* Teaching your dog to *love* to behave
* Consistency, consistency, consistency

David Premack developed the *Premack Principle*. It puts forth "the observation that high-probability behavior reinforces low-probability behavior." Essentially it means this: "Eat your vegetables and you can have dessert." To make this a bit easier to understand in terms of dog training, high-probability behaviors are what the *dog* wants; low-probability behaviors are what *you* want. In this chapter, you learn how to use this principle to get the behaviors you want from your dog.

Eating Your Vegetables First: What You Want

So what do you want from your dog? Think about this—really think. It's not easy, is it? Write it down if you have to. Come up with concrete things you want. If *you* don't know what you want, how the heck is *he* supposed to know? I know dogs are very smart and may seem to be "almost human," but I don't believe dogs (or spouses or children) can really read your mind.

MUTTLEY MEANINGS

The **Premack Principle** states that high-probability behavior reinforces low-probability behavior.

Do you want your dog to sit quietly at the door when the leash is being put on? How about calm behaviors when walking down the street? Perhaps bringing the ball and dropping it at your feet rather than 20 feet away? Wouldn't you like to be able to peacefully sit and watch TV, or prepare his food dish and put it on the floor without being mauled? Maybe you'd like him to stop straining at the leash to get to his doggie pal so he can play? You *can* get all these things and more by finding out what your dog wants—what floats his boat.

After you've thought it over, write down what you want from your dog. Then it's time to figure out and write down what *he* wants.

POOCH POINTERS

Be creative and watch your dog. He'll tell you what he wants. It may change from day to day, hour to hour, and even minute to minute. And that's okay—it will give you more reinforcers to choose from.

Hot Fudge Sundae: What Your Dog Wants

How will you know what your dog wants? Watch him carefully and write down what he enjoys most. Don't think you'll remember it all without writing it down, because you won't. Humor me and write it down anyway. It'll come in handy later.

Your dog might like to sniff; roll in smelly things; sniff; chase toys; play tug; play with other dogs; sniff; go swimming; go for a car ride; go for a walk, jog, or run; play in an open field; sniff; chase ducks, deer, or geese; herd sheep; find small rodents; be petted or massaged; sniff; practice agility; cuddle with you; sniff; get belly rubs; retrieve objects; sniff; eat food; pee on bushes (hopefully yours and not the neighbor's); get attention from you; be groomed (my dogs like to be groomed); and last but not least, sniff.

CANINE CAVEATS

Be sure to pick only those things that you would want to use as reinforcers later. Sock stealing, annoying barking, paper eating, garbage raiding, poop eating, furniture re-arranging or chewing, and general behaviors you don't want don't count and shouldn't be on this list.

Now you have two lists—one with what you want and one with what your dog wants. Now let's put them together.

Making Everyone's Dreams Come True

The great thing about Premack is that your dog will very often learn to enjoy "lima beans"—what you want, be it a stay, loose-leash walking, or being touched or groomed. So not only will she learn to accept a bunch of new things, but if you make what she wants contingent upon doing what you want, you will see an increase of tolerance *and* an increase of appropriate behaviors.

Attention = Sheep Herding

Beau, one of my Border Collies, wanted to herd sheep. However, he thought I was irrelevant and was along only as a taxi driver. When herding sheep, it's important that the dog understand that he and his person are a team. He can't herd sheep without someone telling him what direction to go, and his person can't herd sheep without the dog doing his job.

Beau would drag me to the sheep pen. It was obvious by his inattentiveness to me that I didn't exist in his eyes. If I let him herd sheep anyway, he would ignore me and wouldn't take direction from me.

To teach him to focus on me, I insisted that he give me attention, heeling all the way from the car to the sheep pen. No attention meant no sheep. If he ignored me, I would tie him to a post and leave. If he made movements toward me, I would come back to him. If his eye contact then wavered, I would leave again. There was no punishment, no anger, no letting him herd sheep, and no hard feelings. I just patiently waited for his attention.

It took him four "sheepless" sheep lessons to understand that he had to focus on me if he wanted to herd sheep. When he learned this lesson, he was attentive outside the pen as well as inside.

Does Your Dog Own You?

You can use anything on your "what the dog wants" list to get what you want. Say you want to allow your dog to go swimming. You don't want her to drag you to the lake or pool. Make swimming dependent upon walking to the lake on a loose leash. No loose-leash walking, no swimming. If she doesn't walk nicely on the leash, just put her back in the car, wait for 5 to 10 minutes, and try again. If, after three to four tries, she still hasn't noticed that you're alive, take her back home.

If the weather is very hot, make sure your dog is in a crate in your vehicle and that you have sun reflector sheets draped all over your car. That way the car/van stays cool and you can even leave the windows open.

CANINE CAVEATS

If you give in to your dog for any of these things, then you're reinforcing the wrong behaviors. "Oh, but I drove all this way so that she could swim." Too bad, Bucko. If you're serious about wanting certain behaviors, then don't give in to the unacceptable behaviors you don't want.

In the beginning, you may have to lower your standards a bit. For instance, you may realistically only be able to get two steps of loose-leash walking before racing to the lake. That's okay. You can build that to three steps, then four, and so on. Make those first approximations small, and you will see success.

Becoming a Master Manipulator

I am working with two Beagles. This breed has a natural tendency to have their noses on the ground 24/7, because humans bred in that behavior. So instead of fighting their "Beagle-ness," we worked with it and exploited it. The first week, we asked (okay, we lured … and then asked) for about 1 minute of attention and then let them go be Beagles for about 10 minutes. Then we repeated the process and asked for 2 minutes of attention, and then 10 minutes of being a dog. By lesson number 3, they were both glued to their owners for 15 to 20 minutes at a clip.

The moral? Work *with* your dog, not against her, and you will have the dog of your dreams.

Your dog wants to go out, but you don't want her to jump up and down like an idiot when you try to put on her collar and leash. Ignore her jumping and wait patiently. When she's sitting calmly, put the leash on. If at any time she starts jumping again, stand still and wait. If it takes 15 minutes, so be it. She will very quickly learn that, if she sits quietly, she'll get to go for a walk faster.

The key for Premacking anything is to know what your dog wants and then ask for what you want—be it calm behavior, eye contact, Sits, Downs, Stays, or whatever you want from her.

> **DOGGIE DATA**
>
> Sue's Australian Cattle Dog, Barney, wanted sniffing to be his full-time job, so she put him on a "pay attention to me or you don't get to sniff" program.
>
> Sue insisted on eye contact from Barney from the instant he left the car—she gave him 30 seconds to respond. If he ignored her, back into the car he went. When he made eye contact within 30 seconds, she lowered the time and repeated this until Barney was responding within 3 seconds.
>
> Sue would ask for some heeling, a Sit, or a Down. Then as a reward, she allowed Barney to sniff for a minute. If he didn't respond, he was put back into the car. Pretty soon, Barney was quickly responding to all sorts of cues—and sniffing less!

Added Benefits

Let's say you have a dog who doesn't like to be touched. You can make touching a prerequisite to going outside. No touchy, no outside. Or no touchy, no bally.

You don't have to start with a full body rub. In fact, you shouldn't. Start with one light touch and then give the dog what he wants. Each day, you can add slightly more petting until you're eventually giving the dog a bear hug and he's actually liking the handling.

> **DOGGIE DATA**
>
> Todd's dog Jesse hated to be handled in any way, but loved tennis balls. By lightly touching each and every body part before throwing the ball, over the course of a few months, Todd was able to groom and pet Jesse. In fact, Jesse learned to love petting so much that not only was Todd able to handle his dog, but their entire relationship changed for the better.

The neat thing about Premacking is that the dog will very often learn to enjoy whatever behavior you want. This is what "reinforcing low-probability behavior" means. The less likely of the two behaviors actually comes to seem valuable to the dog. My Sheltie Cody actually likes toenail clipping because I Premacked it with stuff he wanted. Now you have yet another way to reinforce your dog!

A dolphin at SeaWorld was in serious need of fresh water. The only way to accommodate this need was through a stomach tube, but the dolphin had to be trained to accept this within five days, otherwise he was going to die.

The trainers not only taught the dolphin to accept the stomach tube, but they did their job so well that the dolphin ended up *liking* the stomach tube—so much so that he *wanted* it as a reward! How's *that* for the ultimate in Premack?! Did I get your creative juices flowing? What will you train your dog to *love?*

Giving Consistent Cues

Premack can backfire *only* if you're inconsistent. If sometimes you give in and sometimes you hold your ground, then guess what? Premack won't work for you. And your dog will still be pulling you on the leash, sniffing nonstop, or doing all the things that drive you insane. In fact, no dog training will work for you if you're inconsistent. Inconsistency is extremely frustrating for your dog, just as it is for humans.

Think about how your dog feels. He doesn't speak English. Really. You only think he does. So if today "come on" means come, and tomorrow "let's go" means come, and the next day "come" means loose-leash walking, and the day after that "come here" means come … well, you can see how frustrating that can be to your dog and why your dog ignores you a lot of the time.

CANINE CAVEATS

If you're inconsistent in your training and cues, you can't blame your dog when he doesn't do what you want. Well, you can, but deep down, you'll know the truth. Uniformity is the key.

Pop Quiz

1. Come up with a list of 15 things your dog likes. (Don't forget, sock stealing, poop eating, and so on, do not belong on this list.)

2. What is the definition of the Premack Principle?

3. How often do you inadvertently change your cues?

The Least You Need to Know

- If you know what behavior *you* want from your dog, you can get that behavior by rewarding her with something you know *she* wants.
- Before the dog gets what he wants, he must do what you want.
- Using Premacking, the dog will very often learn to enjoy the behavior that you want him to do.
- Consistency is the secret to successful Premacking.

Reinforcements

In This Chapter

- You can be boring or you can be impulsive
- Variety is the spice of life
- Surprise! Here's a ticket to Hawaii!
- Being the best trainer you can be

Behaviorist B. F. Skinner discovered three reinforcement schedules for animal training. Two of them will create a bored, lazy, and non-compliant dog. By using only those two, you may hear your dog say, "Yeah, sure, when I feel like it." But if you use the third variable schedule of reinforcement, you'll be sure to get "Sure! When? Yesterday? No problemo!" Add surprise elements and there is no limit to what you and your dog can accomplish.

Different Reinforcement Schedules

B. F. Skinner was the first to discover how variable reinforcement schedules can increase or decrease specific behaviors. Skinner came upon this marvel of observable fact when he was running out of rat pellets during experiments and the rats still performed behaviors, at a stable rate, for less food. Wahoo!

He called it *schedules of reinforcement,* and it opened up a whole new area of study for him and others in behavioral psychology. The study of it spread to marine mammal trainers and then to dog trainers (and sometimes even to human trainers).

You can use three different types of reinforcement schedules for training: continuous, fixed, and variable. Some are more effective than others in maintaining or advancing behaviors. Some actually kill behaviors.

Continuous Reinforcement

Continuous reinforcement was the original method that Skinner practiced, meaning that a treat was delivered for every correct behavior. This schedule is great for teaching new behaviors.

You can see continuous schedules of reinforcement in your daily life. When you first learned to use a vending machine, it was very reinforcing to put your money in and get a prize. This encouraged you to do it again when you wanted something to eat or drink.

Fixed Reinforcement Slows Down Learning

There are two types of fixed schedules: fixed interval and fixed ratio. With a fixed-interval schedule, the food is fed at specific *times,* rather than for specific behaviors. If your dog does one "sit" in a 20-second period, he gets one treat. If he doesn't sit, he doesn't get a treat. But even if he sits 100 times in 20 seconds, he still gets one treat. One interesting thing that happens is that the dog will pace himself by slowing down the rate of his behavior right after the reinforcer, and speed up again when the time for it gets close.

You call your dog from the backyard to no avail. You call at 10 A.M., you call at noon, and you call at 3 P.M. No doggie. However, at 5 P.M., you call your dog and he comes flying. Why? Because you always feed him his dinner at 5 P.M. He knows that no reinforcement is coming at those other times, so he doesn't come.

Stick to a fixed-interval schedule and you'll get what's called scalloping. Say you're having the dog heel and you give her a treat every five seconds (because we humans are creatures of habit). The dog may, after taking the treat, go off and sniff, and then run back after three or four seconds to get her next "fix."

A different type of fixed schedule is the fixed-ratio schedule, which reinforces the dog after so many behaviors on a regular schedule. The dog sits 3, 6, or 20 times and always gets a cookie after the third, sixth, or twentieth time. The number of behaviors asked for remains the same between reinforcers in a fixed-ratio schedule.

Fixed-interval and fixed-ratio schedules can kill behaviors in dogs as well as humans. Fixed ratios are predictable, and predictability is boring, tedious, dreary, and mind-numbing.

Okay, so you get the point on how predictability kills behavior. What's the answer? Variable reinforcement, of course!

Variable Reinforcement

Skinner also looked at two different types of variable reinforcement schedules: variable ratio and variable interval. A variable ratio means that you change the number of behaviors needed each time. First it takes 3 "sits" to get a treat, then 10, then 1, then 7, and so on.

Variable interval means that you keep changing the time period between reinforcements—first 20 seconds, then 5, then 35, then 10, and so on. As a result, dogs no longer pace themselves, because they can no longer establish a rhythm between behavior and reward.

Both variable ratio and variable interval keep dogs on their toes. But most important, these schedules are very resistant to *behavior extinction*. It makes sense if you think about it. In the dog's mind, if she hasn't gotten a reinforcer for a while, well, it just might come if she does just one more "sit"!

 MUTTLEY MEANINGS

Behavior extinction occurs when a behavior is not reinforced anymore and so the behavior stops.

When the Soda Machine Becomes a Slot Machine

When you put money in a slot machine, you might not win very often, but you never know if and when you'll win again. You also don't know how much you'll win—it could be 25¢ or $500. You just might win the very next time, and if you don't try one more time, you might possibly miss on the score of the century!

This is just the opposite of how a vending machine works. You put your money in and a soda comes out. So what happens if you put your money in and nothing comes out? There are a few options you might consider:

- Walk away

- Put in more money and try one more time

- Find a sledgehammer and beat it to pieces

Now, look at this from your dog's point of view. If you get stuck on a continuous reinforcement schedule and all of a sudden you try to be more variable, your dog's possible reactions could include the following:

- Walk away

- Try to sit again, just to make sure the cookie machine isn't broken

- Bark, whine, or bite in frustration because the cookie machine isn't paying out

Eureka! Variable Reinforcement

In the days before prepackaged rat food, Skinner noticed that he would run low in the middle of an experiment. Because he had to make his own food, he decided that he would reduce the number of reinforcements given for a particular behavior. Skinner discovered that the rats continued to perform their behaviors at a consistent rate. Behold the discovery of schedules of reinforcement!

Using and understanding variable reinforcement schedules are vital in teaching longer and stronger behavior patterns. Gambling casinos know this, which is why they make so much money on slot machines. Think they just made up the idea of slot machines? Think again! They have scientifically determined the optimum reward schedule: they let you win just enough to keep you hooked! Brilliant!

DOGGIE DATA

The most notable role models for positive methods are the trainers at SeaWorld parks. They train a killer whale to stay still for dental work without Novocain, to urinate on cue into a paper cup, to allow blood to be drawn, and many other behaviors needed for animal husbandry. Use punishment on these animals and the trainers will be in danger. They use positive training by necessity.

It takes only nine months to train a new whale, including name recognition, "come" cue, allowing touching and daily animal husbandry (does your dog allow grooming?), eye contact, not eating the trainer or other animals—even prey—plus all of the behaviors needed for the show.

Killer whale taught to target a ball—and leap very high in the air!

Variety: The Spice of Your Dog's Life

Add reinforcement variety to variable reinforcement schedules (interval or ratio) and you're home free for life! Variable reinforcement with reinforcement variety is the strongest schedule for maintaining a behavior.

Variety is just that—variety of reinforcement type. The key is not to use the same old thing to reinforce the dog. Reinforcement variety not only makes strong behaviors, but it also helps enrich the dog's life. Here are some examples of reinforcers you can use:

- **Food:** chicken, cheese, hot dogs, liverwurst, tortellini, steak, chickpeas, kidney beans, liver brownies, kibble, burnt leftovers that no one wants, vegetables, fruit; the list is endless.

- **Toys:** tennis balls, Frisbees, tug toys, Kongs (a Kong is a hard rubber toy with a big hole in it for stuffing yummy treats); anything your dog likes to play with. (Exception: Don't use old shoes or socks as toys, because the dog will get the idea that *all* socks and shoes are toys.)

- **Activities:** swimming, car rides, walks in the woods, tag, chasing you, jogging, hiking, grooming (some dogs *do* like being groomed), playing with other dogs.

- **"Life rewards":** sniffing that pile of poop, rolling in smelly things, playing with sticks, peeing on bushes.

- **Other:** praise, clapping, jumping up and down, cheering, petting gently, petting roughly, just hanging out together.

> **CANINE CAVEATS**
>
> It's too easy to get stuck using food as your only reinforcement type. Variable schedules and variable types of reinforcement require you to use creativity, imagination, and forethought.

These are just a taste of the reinforcements you can use to reward your dog. Be creative and watch your dog to see what she likes.

You might think that applying life rewards, rather than giving the dog a piece of food, will slow down training. True, the session may take a bit longer, but in the long run, the behaviors trained will be learned faster, stay longer, and be stronger.

Adding Surprise Elements

Do you want to be a great trainer? There's a method to the madness, and you need to do very real planning to become a great teacher. It may seem difficult at first, but it becomes simple with practice. It can end up being a way of life for many people because the benefits to the dog and to your relationship are enormous and obvious.

What's more yummy? A plain banana, or a banana with three kinds of your favorite ice cream, plus hot fudge and chocolate sprinkles?

Or how would you feel about packing for a vacation that you think will be to Colonial Williamsburg, and your spouse surprises you with tickets to Hawaii?

Which do you think would be more fun for your dog? Eating the same old dry biscuit 10 times in a row for loose-leash walking, or getting one piece of tortellini, a scratch behind the ears, the chance to chase you, five pieces of hot dog, a short game of tug, and a belly rub for the same loose-leash walking?

The point is to be unpredictable. *Plan* surprise rewards, be generous, be fun, be variable in how and when and how much you reinforce, and you'll have the trained dog of your dreams.

Using the methods in this book, you can go from being a lousy trainer to being a great one. Great trainers ...

- Are good at reinforcing.
- Are quick and have good timing.
- Are generous and use lots of reinforcements.
- Are unpredictable and vary when, how much, and how they apply reinforcers.
- Are variable and use many different types of reinforcers.
- Stop problems before they become locked in as solid behaviors.
- Plan their sessions carefully.
- Recognize small approximations and reward them.
- Keep a log or diary of each behavior being taught.

Pop Quiz

1. Which two schedules of reinforcement create a bored and noncompliant dog?

2. Which two schedules of reinforcement create a dog who will leap tall buildings in a single bound?

3. What is scalloping? (Hint: it isn't the fish.)

4. Have you started to use variable reinforcement while training? Are you seeing better results?

5. If you are seeing better results, give yourself a click and ice cream! If you aren't yet, you may want to plan your sessions before you bring your dog out—not only plan the behaviors, but plan your reinforcers as well.

The Least You Need to Know

- Fixed schedules of reinforcement kill behaviors.
- Variable schedules of reinforcement create stronger behaviors and make training more fun and rewarding for your dog.
- Plan surprise rewards for your dog.
- Design a game strategy to become a great trainer.

Dogs and Your Lifestyle

Think you don't have time to train your dog? In three five-minute sessions per day, you—yes, you—can have the dog of your dreams! In Part 4, you'll see how to introduce your dog to your kids, how to get a new dog situated into your family and home, and how to train your dog while holding down a full-time job. And in case you're having problems, here are some tips for curing your dog's lapses in behavior. You will also learn what the Canine Good Citizen certificate is all about and realize that you are most likely closer to earning that than you think!

Adding a Dog to Your Household

Chapter 15

In This Chapter

- Your dog's own domain: crate training
- Potty training
- Good things happen when he's around
- Spit, spat—resource guarding and fights

Adding a dog to your family takes patience and strategic planning. It also takes a real commitment to remain calm and positive and to not forget *your* training of doggie body language.

Adding a second dog (or third, or fourth …) is *not* easy; and at times during the beginning stages, you may want to kick yourself in the head for doing it. However, most of us who have multiple-dog households do survive and actually continue to add more and more, even though we swear at the time, "I will *never* do it again!"

Crate Training

Teaching your dog to love his crate is one of the best things you can do for your new best friend. Your dog will have to be crated many times in his life—for grooming, vet visits, or if he ever gets lost and is picked up by animal control.

Crate training is essential for younger dogs or rescue dogs to help them not soil or eat the house. If you don't want your dog jumping in bed with you at 2 A.M. ready to play, you'll need to put him in the crate. You can also crate your young pup when company comes until you can train him not to jump on visitors.

The Benefits of Crate Training

The benefits of crate training (to both you and the dog) are numerous:

- Makes housetraining easier—be it house soiling or chewing.

- Gives the dog a safe, secure place to "get away from it all."

- Manages the dog when you are busy and can't pay attention to her. This includes when visitors come, when you're leaving for work, when you're cooking dinner and the dog wants to play, and so on.

- Helps you manage a multiple-dog household.

- Enables your dog to cope with vet and groomer visits, where she will be crated.

- Makes traveling with your dog easier, safer, and less stressful for both of you.

Crate-Training Instructions

Break up crate training into several different sessions. Before you start the first session, have lots of treats on hand (my definition of "lots" is about three baggies filled with pea-size treats). Keep the door open and follow these steps:

1. Throw a handful of treats into the crate.

2. Stand back (so as not to pressure the dog) and let him go into the crate on his own.

3. When he is done eating the treats, throw in more.

Pretty soon, the dog will just stay in the crate, waiting for you to throw in more treats. This usually takes about 10 to 15 minutes.

DOGGIE DATA

If you do your research well, you can find a breeder who actually crate trains all the puppies before they leave the nest.

In the next session, throw in a few cookies to "review," and then wait for the dog to go into the crate on his own. Then throw in wads of cookies as a reward (as opposed to a bribe) for going into the crate. Then follow these steps:

1. Call him out of the crate and then *look* at the crate (don't say anything yet).

2. When he goes back into the crate, reward him again heavily.

3. Repeat the preceding two steps five or six times.

In your third session, follow these steps:

1. Go over to the crate and look at it (still don't say anything).

2. When he goes back into the crate, reward him heavily.

3. Repeat this four or five times.

4. Then, as he is going into the crate (not before—pair the word with the behavior), say "crate" or "place" or whatever you want your word to be for telling the dog to go to his crate.

5. Reward heavily when he goes into his crate.

6. Repeat about five times.

In your fourth session, repeat steps 2 and 4 from the preceding list. Then say the word "crate" *before* he goes in, to see if he understands. If he goes into the crate, give him a mega jackpot of treats! Repeat this four to five times and then end the session.

At the fifth session, you'll start closing the door while the dog is comfortable going into his crate. Close the door for about five seconds, while he is still eating the last jackpot you gave him. Before he is done eating, open the door. Let him come out of the crate. Repeat a few times.

In later sessions, start gradually—and I mean gradually (a few extra seconds at a time; use a timer to keep you on track)—keeping the door closed for longer periods of time. You can even sit next to the crate while dropping food into it.

CANINE CAVEATS

You must keep this slow. If at any time the dog whines, you have gone on too long. If the dog whines or barks, you cannot let her out of the crate until she is quiet. If you let the dog out of the crate while she is whining, she will learn to whine in her crate—a mega no-no!

You can also use a special toy that he gets only while in his crate. I like Kong toys stuffed with nut butter or other gushy foods to keep them occupied. Continue to build up the duration that your dog can stay in the crate to at least a full minute before you start to leave the room.

After you have mastered this, in future sessions, you can start leaving the room. Follow these steps:

1. Start by doing this for one second. Leave the room and instantly come back.

2. Reward the dog for being quiet and open the crate door.

3. Then leave for two seconds, then three, then four, and so on, *always setting the dog up to not whine.* Keep him busy with a frozen stuffed Kong (stuffed with gooey foods, such as peanut butter, cream cheese, and some treats) or a nice, meaty, raw bone.

 CANINE CAVEATS

Never, never use the crate as punishment. If your dog is being "bad," put him in his crate, but do it gently and unemotionally and give him a treat anyway. Putting him away *after* he has been "bad" teaches the dog *nothing,* but it keeps you from killing him!

You can also feed the dog his dinner in the crate, which will speed along his acclimation to it. Repeat all the preceding steps until you can leave your dog in his crate for hours at a time. This will not take as long as it sounds. I crate-trained one dog, whom the owner said couldn't be crate-trained, in 45 minutes.

Security Tips

You can do a few things to ensure that your dog comes home safe and sound if she ever gets lost:

- **Microchips:** Most veterinarians can insert a small microchip in the shoulder-blade area. Most veterinarians, rescue groups, and shelters have a scanner and can scan the dog to get your contact information.

- **Tattoos:** A tattoo goes on the inner thigh. Two registries keep information on tattooed dogs. Be aware, however, that many rescue organizations will not look for a tattoo, and they are harder to see on longhaired dogs.

- **Photos:** Always have a current photo on hand in case you need to put up flyers.

- **Emergency info:** When you are traveling with the dog, keep information in the car or your wallet in case you have an accident. Include contact numbers of friends who will take the dog, name of veterinarian, any medical information needed, and any behavioral issues the dog may have.

The Bathroom Is Outside

Above all, know that housetraining is a human issue, not a dog issue. We are the ones who want and need the dog to use the outside latrine. They don't care at all. It is imperative to give the dog a great deal of access to the outside. If a dog is left alone in the house for long periods of time, she will have no choice but to eliminate inside.

Have patience with your dog. You wouldn't yell at your child for soiling his or her diaper, so don't yell at your dog. Yelling might make you feel better, but think what association you are creating: squatting around you is dangerous. Forget about "catching her in the act." Just ignore it and move on with your life.

Knowing When to Go

So what is your option? Be smarter than she is! Note how soon after eating, sleeping, napping, playing, and drinking she usually "goes." If, for example, she messes five minutes after eating, then take her outside three minutes after eating.

Learn your dog's signs that he has to go. He is not some little kid who can cram his fists into his crotch, bend his knees, and look desperate. Common signs of "I gotta go!" are circling, whining, frantic look on his face, bent tail, hunched butt area, enlarged anus, and sniffing. If you are playing with him when you see any of these signs, then stop playing and take him out; otherwise, you're asking for a puddle.

> **DOGGIE DATA**
>
> Humans have opposable thumbs that can open doors. Dogs do not. Ergo, dogs cannot open doors. So you'll just have to get up and take the dog out!

You can also teach your dog to go to the door when she needs to eliminate. As you cross the threshold, say "Outside." Do this for a few weeks. Then when you think she has to go, ask her "Outside?" and she will probably go to the door.

I also find that some dogs like to ring a bell to let you know that they want to go out. For some reason I have yet to figure out, toy dogs will learn faster this way that the bathroom is outside.

- Hang a bell on a string at nose level from the doorknob.

- Put a tiny dab of peanut butter on the bell and encourage your dog to lick it (causing the bell to ring). Click and treat when they do and instantly say "Outside" and take the dog outside.

- Repeat a bunch of times until the peanut butter is gone and they are still ringing the bell and you are still taking them outside.

Most dogs learn this within a few minutes—ring the bell = go outside.

Heavily reward the dog *outside* when she does her business and in the same spot where she went. *Do not* reinforce her after you're back in the house unless you want her to mess the house. When you can't be watching her, put her in a crate (my recommendation), in an exercise pen, or on an easily cleanable floor. If she does mess on carpeting, be sure to clean it instantly and thoroughly. Otherwise, that spot will forever smell like the bathroom to her.

CANINE CAVEATS

Some dogs may lie—they will ring the bell to let you think they have to go outside, but they really don't need to go, they just want to. A great way to handle this is to say, "I'll be right there, honey!" Then wait a few seconds. If the dog ends up doing something else, you know that he didn't really need to go. If he continues to hang out by the door, then you know that he wasn't lying.

If you can't seem to read your dog's signs, tether her to you with a six-foot leash. This will force you to pay closer attention to her, and you'll be able to get her out faster, with fewer accidents.

False Alarms and Accidents

There may be times when you take your dog out and she won't do her business. Then she comes back into the house and messes at your feet. Please don't get angry with her. That is just counterproductive. The next time you take her out, wait longer until she goes. If it takes 10 minutes, it takes 10 minutes. Bring a book, call your mother, or practice the multiplication tables in your head, but *do not* bring that dog back into the house until she is empty.

If after 15 minutes she still hasn't gone, put her in her crate, wait for 10 minutes, and try again. Continue to do this until she goes outside. Reward her heavily when she finally goes where you want her to go.

If she does mess in the house, grab the nearest newspaper, roll it up, and hit yourself over the head while chanting, "I forgot to watch my dog, I forgot to watch my dog." If your dog laughs, praise her.

When a Second Dog Comes Home

The best way to introduce a new dog to an existing dog is to do it in a neutral place that neither dog feels is "his." Off-leash is better, and you should add scads of food to the mix. You can hand-feed each dog simultaneously and also dump tons of food on the ground. If your dog guards food, be careful; throw the food in opposite directions to avoid any arguments.

Why would you feed the dogs together? Have you forgotten Pavlov already? Add positive associations for both dogs from the very beginning and you'll have a better chance of success.

I think the best way to introduce a new dog is to take both dogs for a nice long walk together on a trail or in the woods. If you are rescuing a new dog, ask the shelter if you can do this at least two or three times before bringing your new dog home. This way, you will know ahead of time if the new dog will get along with your existing dog and it will also give *you* more time to be with the new guy to make sure he is the right dog for you.

If you're getting a puppy, you can do this as well. Sniffing and "hunting" are great communal activities; plus, outside is bigger than inside and the dogs will feel less pressure outside. Less pressure means calmer behaviors, which in turn means better associations for all involved.

If you see a squabble, you must *not* punish either of the dogs. If you do, you're setting them up for a lifetime of hatred—think Hatfields and McCoys. You already learned in Chapter 3 what will happen if you punish, so please avoid this at all costs.

Feeding two dogs at the same time, keeping them equidistant from each other and the handler. Feed so that the dogs' heads are turned away from each other to avoid conflicts.

(Photo by P. Dennison)

No, You Can't Have It!

Food and resource guarding are common problems in a multi-dog household. The resources a dog can guard can be you, other family members, toys, beds (yours and his), food bowls, crates, and even furniture.

Positive Solutions to Resource Guarding

The positive solution is to do the following:

- Reinforce the more *dominant* dog for ignoring the subordinate dog. You can click and treat the dominant dog for attention while the subordinate dog is being a pest. Or you can click and toss treats to the dominant dog while you pet the subordinate dog.

> **MUTTLEY MEANINGS**
>
> **Dominant** means assertive or pushy, not aggressive. Some dogs (as well as some people) don't know how to take "no" for an answer and will continue to push or be obnoxious.

- Reinforce the more dominant dog for allowing the subordinate dog to get attention.

- Reinforce any and all "pro-social" behaviors such as gentle tail wagging, playing, play bows, and mutual grooming.

- Feed the subordinate dog first, so that the dominant dog learns a little patience.

If you reinforce the dominant dog for being dominant, then what will happen? He will become completely overbearing and out of control.

Change, change, change everything! Switch blankets, crates, positions, food bowls—anything that your dog normally uses. It's imperative that you don't allow territory to be established and protected through your predictability. Reinforce any calming signals that you see because these are what stop squabbles from happening.

To avoid having one of your dogs become possessive of you, learn to position yourself into a triangle with you as the tip of it and the dogs as the base of it. Many dogs don't want to "share," but it's important that they learn to—for everyone's sake. This takes a bit of maneuvering on your part. Whenever I get a new dog, for at least a month I make sure that I position myself so that no one is guarding me.

> **DOGGIE DATA**
>
> Shadow is the pushiest dog in my pack of four. I used to feed him first because I was under the common misconception that "you should always feed the dominant dog first." That was a big mistake. I would feed him and then try to feed the other dogs. He would view *all* of the food as his. I had to constantly be on the lookout to stop potential fights.
>
> As soon as I started feeding him last, all the potential arguments stopped and he now waits patiently for his turn. Why should this be so? Because he now sees the other dogs being fed as a cue that his is coming up soon, and he's actually much calmer when dinner time or "cookie time" rolls around.

You can also use this triangle position to teach dogs each other's names. Say "Rover," and then give Rover a treat. Then say "Fifi," and give Fifi a treat. Repeat a zillion times. This will come in handy when you want Rover to "stay" there and Fifi to "come." Just wait until you have three or four or more dogs! You'll be grateful that you taught them this.

Splitting Up

Dogs split other dogs to push them away, to guard things, or to avoid conflict from what they perceive as too-rough play. You can use it effectively yourself, provided that you're watching your dogs carefully. You must split at the earliest sign of conflict that you can see. It takes a great deal of practice to accomplish this and be successful, but it's well worth it in the long run.

When you split in between them, if they then move away from each other, be sure to reinforce both dogs for parting. This will help you to be successful in avoiding problems in the future.

Make sure to crate-train both dogs and use this to your benefit. Spend quality time with each dog alone, and then when you do have both of them out together, make sure that good things always happen around the other dog. If you don't have time to pay attention to both of them, put them in their crates. This will give them some good downtime to relax.

How to split the dogs if one gets pushy.
(Photo by P. Dennison)

It's stressful even with the best mix of two personalities, so be sure to give both dogs some quiet time. On average, it usually takes about four to six months to have complete harmony in the house. Sometimes you may get lucky and it takes only a few days, but that's not the norm. Keep each of your sessions with both dogs short, positive, and successful.

If one dog is very pushy toward the other one, be sure to split and reinforce both dogs—the pushy one for going "over there and lying down," and the patient one for putting up with the pushy one. As you split, you can even say, "Excuse me." I did this with my dogs and ended up being able to say those words and they would split themselves.

It's very important for you to stay calm during all introductions and future training sessions. If you're stressed, what association do you think the two dogs will make? That's right—the dogs will get stressed because *you're* stressed. Even if they do have a "fight," it's vital that you remain calm.

Dangerous Squabbles?

Most squabbles are not serious. You may see teeth flashing and hear scary noises, and you may think that they're killing each other. Don't be alarmed—be calm. Watch them carefully and you'll most likely see that no contact is made, and even if contact is made, most of the time they leave only spit and no punctures.

The most important things you can do are the following:

- Remain calm.
- Don't yell or hit or say *anything*.
- Split between them if you can.
- *Run* out of the room fast! The dogs will see you running away (dogs are attracted to movement) and will most likely follow you to see where you're going.

Most "arguments" last only a few seconds, although it seems that they go on forever. Yelling or hitting will incite them to aggress for longer periods of time and with more intensity. Silence is the way to go until all is calm. Then, if you want to, you can go in the bathroom, shut the door, and scream all you like. The next time, just be more cognizant of what they're doing, so that you can stop conflicts before they escalate.

What Am I Doing Wrong?

If you see that their squabbles are increasing in duration and intensity, put both dogs in their crates, sit down, and ask yourself these questions:

- Have I been punishing them for arguments? Punishment includes yelling and hitting.
- Have I been giving them enough downtime and alone time?
- Am I setting them up to fail by pushing them or forcing them to be pals?

- Am I watching them carefully, stopping conflicts before they start?

- Am I reinforcing all pro-social and friendly behaviors?

- Am I assuming that the original dog has to be "top dog" because she's been here longer, and forcing the new dog into the role of subordinate?

- Do the dogs view me as their own personal chew toy and are they guarding me, creating the fights?

POOCH POINTERS

Humans have arguments all the time that mean nothing, and so do dogs. When we fight, we scream and yell, which is frightening to dogs because they're not humans and they don't understand what we're saying. Their noises and their big white teeth are scary to us because we're not dogs and we don't understand what they're saying, either.

Be sure that you aren't the cause of their fights or contributing to the intensity. If you *really* feel that you need to break them up physically, then walk up slowly (if you run in screaming, the fight may take a turn for the worse), you and someone else need to grab both dogs by the back legs, and pull them apart as gently and calmly as you can. They will usually look back in surprise and then you'll be able to redirect them to a safer area.

Is Everybody Okay?

After the dogs are separated and everyone is calm, check them over for any punctures. You can take care of most punctures yourself— just clean the wound, check it over the next day or two, and stop worrying. Even when dogs are playing, punctures can happen, so there's no need to freak out.

Continue to make sure that good things happen when they're together, ignore any squabbles, and heavily reinforce any pro-social, friendly behaviors, and your best friends will be buddies for life.

> **CANINE CAVEATS**
>
> When breaking up a dog fight, *never* grab them by the neck or collar—you're just asking to get bitten. If you're lucky enough to have another person with you, each of you should take hold of a dog's hind legs and tail simultaneously, and move a large distance away so that you can contain the dogs. If you're by yourself, take control of the dog who seems to have the upper hand.

Pop Quiz

1. Why is it a good idea to reinforce all pro-social behavior when adding a new dog?

2. If your dogs have a tiff, what's the best thing for you to do?

3. Have you crate-trained all your dogs using the methods listed in this chapter?

4. Are you fluent in reading your dog(s)' body language? If so, you'll be able to stop problems way before they start. Review Chapter 5.

The Least You Need to Know

- Make sure all your dogs are crate-trained so that you can manage them better when you first bring a new dog home.

- Housetraining is an essential skill—but one that is driven by your needs and desires rather than your dog's.

- When you introduce a new dog to existing dogs, avoid any and all punishments, so that only positive associations are made between the two dogs. Watch them both carefully and reinforce all calm, playful behaviors.

- Most squabbles are harmless, but if they do escalate, look to yourself and your management of the two dogs.

Kids and Dogs

In This Chapter

- Can you handle a kid and a dog together?
- How to train the kids
- What will you do with Rover when the baby comes?
- How to love, cherish, and honor (your dog)

You're watching television and you see this really cute commercial with a young child sitting on the ground, giggling, with a million puppies climbing all over him. The puppies are having fun and the kid is having fun. You look over to your spouse with tears in your eyes and say, "Honey, let's get Lily a puppy."

Think first, long and hard, and then think again. Then think one more time. Kids and dogs don't generally go well together. Kids like to grab, poke, hit, and jump. Puppies and dogs have sharp teeth and claws. Kids are easily scared and have delicate skin. Furthermore, moms are usually busy with kid stuff and don't have time to properly train the puppy. This chapter explores all the issues involved when kids and dogs interact.

A Match Made in Heaven or ...?

If your child is very young, you'll need to manage both the child and the dog a great deal, making sure their needs are both met. As the puppy grows—and grow they do, much faster than we slow-developing primates—the adolescent dog may become too big and overwhelming for your still-tiny child.

DOGGIE DATA

I thought this was one of the most brilliant and impressive ideas I had ever seen with regard to not yielding to "kid pressure": Richard's teenage daughters were bugging him to get a dog. He said to them, "No problem, but this is what you have to do first. For two weeks you must stand outside four times per day for 15 minutes, no matter what the weather. If you complain or try to pass the job onto someone else—no dog." After about three days, the kids started complaining and tried to shirk their responsibility. Needless to say, Richard did not get a dog.

If you have older children, as the puppy grows, the kids will take less and less interest in her—forget that they said, "I *promise* I'll take the dog out, feed her dinner, clean up her messes. I'll do everything! Please, pretty please!!"

You and I both know how long *that* will last. In about two days, you'll start to hear, in a plaintive whine: "Mom, the puppy is biting me (stealing my toys, pooping on my homework, eating my homework)"; "I have to do my homework so I don't have time to take her out"; and so on. When you get a dog, you're acquiring a living, breathing being with huge needs. It's incredibly rewarding to raise a puppy, but be aware—it's not for the faint of heart.

Feeding and Housetraining

What does it mean to add a puppy to your household, along with your existing children? First, it means feedings three times per day, and cleaning up messes several times per day for anywhere from a month or two to a year. Some dogs are housetrained almost instantly, and other puppies or dogs just don't get it.

Because punishment will only make housetraining harder, there's nothing much you can do to speed up the process. Just as with toddlers, some puppies have the neurological development to "hold it" at an earlier age than others. You may get lucky and get one of the dogs who is housetrained at 16 weeks, or you may get one who's simply incapable of being reliable until 10 or even 12 months of age.

> **CANINE CAVEATS**
>
> An absolute cardinal rule: *never* buy a dog for a child; buy a dog for *yourself.* If you're not willing or able to assume 100 percent responsibility for that dog, then *don't get a dog!*

Playtime

Be aware that the puppy's capacity for play is going to be *a lot* more than yours. She's going to be just like a pesky little kid who never wants to stop. This is normal and something that you, as the adult, need to understand, prepare for, and accommodate.

> **POOCH POINTERS**
>
> When dogs play, they body slam, growl, bite, and rearrange furniture. Dogs do *not* play Parcheesi. Puppies need vigorous play to develop into physically and mentally healthy dogs. You can limit the venues and rules of the play, but you must allow plenty of opportunities for it. If you get a puppy and want him to just sleep in the corner and be cute, he will never grow into a well-adjusted dog.

Proper Supervision and Doggie Daycare

It's a fact of life that puppies and dogs bite—it's natural and it's how they interact with their world, especially in the beginning. Human toddlers also go through a stage where they learn about their environment by putting things in their mouth, or sometimes biting.

You must constantly supervise any activity that includes children and your dog so that no one—dog or child—gets hurt. There will be accidents no matter how careful you are, and some items will get chewed and some skin will get nipped.

If you work full-time, you must find either a doggie daycare or a dog walker to come in several times per day. It's not unthinkable to get a puppy while you work, but it's as cruel to leave a puppy alone all day as it is to leave a tiny infant alone all day. If you ask around, you'll find someone in your neighborhood who is available during the day and willing to babysit your pup. You can also find a doggie daycare for the first few months you have the puppy and then gradually leave the dog home for longer periods of time, while having a dog walker come in a few times.

Although crate training is essential, you can't expect a pup to stay in the crate all day. I recommend getting an exercise pen, also called an "X-pen." (You can get a pen from one of the pet-supply, mail-order catalogs for approximately $30 to $60, depending on the size.) You can put "safe" toys in it. If you're busy when you get home, at least you can put the puppy in it and she can move around a bit without getting into any trouble.

POOCH POINTERS

Some people "puppy-proof" a room and then leave their pup loose in it, totally unsupervised. Such attempts generally fail. Think putting your puppy in a completely tiled bathroom is safe? Think again! You may find that he figures out how to chew the door or eat the linoleum floor.

Teaching Your Children

Okay, so you've decided that you *do* have "the right stuff"—the dedication, wherewithal, nerves of steel, patience of a saint, no carpeting, stock in a paper towel company, and the determination—to train this dog from day one, so that he never ends up in a shelter. You've done extensive research and found a highly recommended breeder and trainer, and you bring home the puppy of your dreams (not, one hopes, the puppy of your nightmares).

Children as young as three-and-a-half years old can be taught to train the dog along with you. This teaches the child responsibility, maturity, appreciation, and affection for a fellow creature. Having your child train your dog teaches the dog that kids are good things, and not chew toys or littermates. "The family that trains their dog together, enjoys their dog together."

One of my students has a Rhodesian Ridgeback puppy, Liam, who loved to knock her three boys to the ground and sit on them. The boys didn't think that was funny, although the dog obviously did. We taught the boys to train the dog. Within two weeks, the dog stopped mauling them and was responding correctly to their cues for good behavior.

A five-year-old girl training her Boxer puppy to sit.
(Photo by P. Dennison)

R.E.S.P.E.C.T.

You can, should, and *must* train your children to respect your new dog as a living, breathing creature and not as a stuffed animal that can be replaced. Any child of any age should be taught to show consideration for the new family member.

If you can, bring your well-mannered children to puppy class and beginner's class and have them train along with you. If the school doesn't allow children, teach them at home the exercises you learned in school.

Do's and Don'ts

Remember that TV commercial you saw with the happy puppies and giggling child that started this whole venture? Commercials are not real life, and there are some very real do's and don'ts that have serious ramifications if you mix them up.

Do's:

- Supervise kids and dogs every second of every day.

- Pair positives for the dog when the kids are around.

- Reinforce your children for being nice to the dog.

- Look for opportunities to reinforce the dog for tolerating rough handling by your kids.

- Teach your kids to be calm and gentle.

- Look at each new child you meet as a training opportunity, to continue the desensitization process.

Don'ts:

- Never let your dog discipline your child. Watch your child to make sure he or she isn't being obnoxious to the dog. Watch your dog for signs of stress and call them away from each other if your dog gets nervous.

- Never let your child discipline your dog. Remember that associative learning is happening all the time. We certainly don't want your dog to have bad feelings toward your children.

- Never leave your child and dog unsupervised.

- Never let your children overstimulate the dog. Running around screaming in a high-pitched voice can actually stimulate prey drive. It's not fair to ask the dog to be calm under those circumstances *unless* you systematically desensitize him to screaming kids. Put the dog away if you're too busy to train him at that moment to accept the children.

Is it doable to have children and a dog? Of course it is, but don't bend to kid pressure or the American Dream pressure of having two and a half kids, two cars, a house, and a dog. Get a dog because *you* want one, and be sure you'll have time for him for the next 15 to 17 years.

POOCH POINTERS

If you look at training your dog as a chore, you're approaching it with the wrong attitude. This should be a labor of love and just as important, if not more so, as taking your kids to soccer practice. The dog will learn many skills needed to make him a great adult, and you'll also have the family pet of your dreams.

Pregnant Pause

You have a dog and find out you're pregnant. Congratulations! As soon as you know you're expecting, you must start training your dog to accept the new baby. Don't wait until the baby is born to start desensitizing him—that's way too late.

Can you have a dog and a new baby? Yes, but you need to plan ahead and train ahead. If you don't have the dog yet and know you'll want a dog and a child, my wholehearted recommendation is to wait until your child is between five and eight years of age. In fact, most reputable breeders won't sell you a dog unless your kids are in this age group. And for good reason: it is hard to raise kids and dogs at the same time, and these breeders don't want their dogs to end up in a shelter or with behavioral problems.

Let's say you don't have kids (but are planning on a family someday) and want to adopt a dog from a shelter or rescue group. *Before* bringing her home, make sure that the dog you select is good with kids. It would be horrible to get a dog now, get pregnant in a few years, and then find out that your best friend hates kids.

Changes for the Dog

Your dog will have to get comfortable with many things when the new baby arrives. Here are some of the more obvious ones:

- New smells

- Sights—baby doing baby things, plus all the paraphernalia that goes along with a baby

- Sounds of crying and whining

- Baby things all over the house that aren't new chew toys

Most of the dog bites in this country happen to small children, by their families' own dogs.

Here are some less obvious but equally important changes that your dog can expect and you *must* train her to accept:

- Mommy and Daddy being cranky and tired and perhaps overwhelmed with the new baby.

- Less attention, exercise, training, and petting than she's used to.

- Being crated more often than she's used to.

- The dog herself being cranky and tired because, of course, she'll wake up every time you do to check on the baby.

- Seeing a toddling baby and not mistaking the child for a prey object—to be killed or played with roughly.

Protecting the Dog from Junior

Baby doesn't understand that your living, breathing dog is not a stuffed toy, and a toddler might now understand that the dog isn't a stuffed toy. Babies and young children don't have the cognitive capabilities to comprehend that the pain they inflict does, in fact, hurt. (If you don't have one yet, you'll find this out, too—personally.) It's your job as the adult to make sure that the baby doesn't hurt the dog. An otherwise "nice" dog is extremely unlikely to hurt the baby, unless he is severely provoked.

Preparing Your Dog for the Baby

So what do you need to do the *instant* you find out you're pregnant? Train, train, train! Please don't suddenly wake up in your eighth month and remember that your dog needs training. Chaining your dog in the backyard for the rest of her life, or even for a brief time, is not an answer—ever.

Work on the foundation behaviors in Parts 2 and 3, specifically eye contact, loose-leash walking, name recognition, "come" with distractions, long "down stays" (build up to about five minutes—or the approximate time it takes to change or feed a baby), proper door etiquette, ignoring dropped food, and accepting rough handling.

After the baby comes home, practice a lot of team training—where one of you feeds the baby and the other one reinforces the dog for being calm. You can train "sit stays" or "down stays" while diapering. Above all, make sure that nothing bad happens to the dog in the presence of the baby.

CANINE CAVEATS

Never punish your dog for being too rough or upset when the baby cries. Just calmly remind the dog to stay and give him something else to do. Watch him carefully, make sure he always remains calm, and reinforce any and all calm behaviors.

You may even want to board the dog for a week when you first come home with the new baby. That way, when the dog comes home, you'll have gotten into a routine that you're comfortable with and can happily include the dog. Be sure that you've already boarded your dog a few times with a reputable kennel so that being kenneled will not be traumatic to her. You don't need her crazed when she comes home to you and the new baby.

Having a child and a dog is not impossible, and is in fact easy when you get the hang of it. Most childhood recollections humans have include the dog we grew up with, so please feel free to let your children have those same great memories.

> **DOGGIE DATA**
>
> One of the major differences between positive training and other methods is that the positive method builds a strong bond between you and the dog and teaches the dog that smaller, weaker things (such as himself) are treated kindly, and are never physically or verbally corrected or punished. A dog trained this way is very likely to welcome the newest member of the household with a happy, nurturing spirit, because you taught him that small, helpless beings are to be cared for, not dominated. On the other hand, if you use punishment on your dog, he'll see that force is the way to control his environment and will be more likely to transfer that violence and ugly behavior onto the new baby.

The Canine Bill of Rights

Your dog should have as many rights as your child. When you buy or rescue a dog, you're making a commitment to care for and train that dog to the best of your abilities for his lifetime. If you can't afford the time or money needed for his health care and training, you may want to rethink getting a dog. When you take on the commitment, I hope you will promise to do the following:

- Provide a place in your daily life for the 15-plus years where he will live, no matter what your life changes may be.

- Provide quality food and clean water.

- Provide proper socialization.

- Provide shelter from hot and cold weather.

- Provide clear, concise, *positive* training.

- Provide good health care and regular grooming.

- Provide daily physical exercise and mental stimulation and enrichment.

- Provide the time and dedication to find proper solutions if the dog develops health or behavioral problems.

In this throwaway society, dogs seem to get the short end of the stick. They can't speak for themselves to tell us their requirements and fears, so we must anticipate and be aware of them. Dogs are social animals, as are humans. To make them live their lives alone in a backyard is like making you live in solitary confinement. You'd go crazy. I'm sure you know dogs who are isolated like this, who bark incessantly, lunge, pace, wear huge ruts in the dirt, and spend their lives alone with virtually no socialization, positive mental and physical stimulation, or companionship.

We owe it to our dogs to take care of them in the best possible way. If you don't have time to train your dog, get a stuffed animal instead.

Pop Quiz

1. If you already have kids, have you thought long and hard and *honestly* about how much time you have to devote to the new dog?

2. Have you researched your breed(s) of choice thoroughly? Do you understand that not all dogs make great family pets with young children?

3. Have you reviewed Chapter 5 on body language? You'll need to do this to avoid problems. You'll be able to see if your dog is getting stressed, and get the kid to come away before the situation ends in a bite.

The Least You Need to Know

- Avoid succumbing to "kid pressure" to get a dog if *you* aren't ready to take full responsibility.
- Never punish your dog around your child—make positive associations only.
- The moment you find that you're pregnant, start training your dog to be ready for the changes the baby will bring.
- You owe it to your dog to honor your lifetime commitment to him despite changes in your life.

Solutions to "Bad" Behaviors

Chapter 17

In This Chapter

- Are you accidentally reinforcing bad behaviors?
- "What's on top of the house?" (Roof!)
- Jumpin' Jack Flash
- Love at first bite
- Attention deficit dog disorder

I have to confess, I personally trained my own dogs to commit all sorts of obnoxious behaviors before I knew better. I trained my Sheltie, Noel, to bark for four hours without taking a breath (you'd think dogs would get hoarse, wouldn't you?) and I also taught her to bark incessantly while I prepared her dinner. I taught my other Sheltie, Cody, to hate his dumbbell, and I allowed Cody to teach Beau and Shadow to fence chase (to run along the fence line while barking). Then I allowed Beau to teach Shadow and Mollie to counter surf (when the dog puts his paws up on the counter and "surfs" around, looking for the goodies people left for him).

Will I ever stop teaching my dogs bad behaviors? Probably not, because to err is human, and to forgive, canine. But I never blame the dogs, because I know that I'm the one who trained them. I stop it as soon as I see something happening and never let it get too "bad."

You, Too, Can Teach Your Dog Really Obnoxious Behaviors!

One of the hardest things to comprehend is that dogs are avid students and quickly learn *exactly* what you teach them. The problem is that humans teach them the wrong behaviors! Not on purpose, of course, but humans do it nonetheless.

Day after day, week after week, year after year, I see people *repeatedly reinforcing what they don't want!* Then they get angry at the dog, perhaps thinking that they have a stupid or stubborn dog. In reality, the dog is actually quite smart and is doing exactly what she was trained to do.

> **CANINE CAVEATS**
>
> Behavior that's reinforced will be repeated. What you may not think of as being reinforcing—hitting, yelling, jerking the leash, attention for bad behaviors—is still *reinforcing for the dog.* If the only time you interact with your dog is to reprimand him, your dog will continue to perform "bad" behaviors to get your attention.

It's not up to you to decide what's reinforcing (or punishing) to your dog—it's your dog's choice. One of my own dogs—Beau—*hates* tortellini and acts like I am trying to poison him, yet Cody would kill for tortellini. I've seen some dogs who love to be sprayed in the face with water and other dogs who find this very punishing.

If it suppresses behavior, it's a punishment. If it increases behavior, it's a reinforcer. Don't forget, though, that although punishment does in fact suppress behavior, it doesn't eliminate it. It may stop the behavior for a short time, but the behavior always comes back.

> **POOCH POINTERS**
>
> My preference is to reinforce "good" behaviors that are incompatible with "bad" ones. For instance, sitting is incompatible with jumping. Have an active dog who climbs the walls? Lying down is incompatible with rearranging the furniture.

The following sections discuss some of the behaviors that are probably on your list and what you can do about them.

Bark! Bark! Bark!

Your dog barks incessantly and you ignore him up to a point. Then *you* start barking (yelling) along with the dog, thus reinforcing the dog's barking. Yahoo! Barking is a very hard behavior to stop because there are so many triggers for it. Real or imagined noises, sights, smells, other animals, kids, and fast movements are just a few of the eight zillion prompts for barking. If your lifestyle won't support a dog that barks, do your research to make sure you don't pick a breed that was bred to bark!

Why Dogs Bark

Some dogs learn to use barking to get your attention. Many dogs bark because (it seems, anyway) they like to hear themselves talk. Shetland Sheepdogs bark at the footfall of a squirrel from two days ago. Some dogs bark out of stress, arousal, or even boredom (which can also be stressful). And some breeds, such as Beagles, Akbash, Great Pyrenees, Anatolian Shepherd Dogs, Nova Scotia Duck Tolling Retrievers, and Lhasa Apsos were specifically bred to bark as part of their jobs (such as herding, hunting, and guarding).

Barking Solutions

As hard as this may seem, the best thing to do is to completely ignore the dog. Walk out of the room, put earplugs in, do whatever you have to do to not react to your dog. Then after five seconds to five minutes of no barking (depending on the length of time the dog was barking), reinforce the dog for the quiet behavior. The longer the dog barks, the longer the quiet behavior should be. Reinforce too soon after five minutes of barking, and that will be what you'll get more of.

If you give in and respond to the dog's barking after, let's say, three minutes, then you've just reinforced three minutes of barking. If you then try again and blow your cool after 10 minutes, you've now reinforced 10 minutes of barking. You get the picture.

> **CANINE CAVEATS**
>
> Reducing or even eliminating barking from the dog's behavior repertoire is not impossible; it just isn't the easiest "bad" behavior to get rid of, especially if you've been reinforcing it in the past.

No matter the situation, as long as you know your dog will react, set him up to be quiet. If he barks in crowds, stay farther away and reinforce quiet behaviors. If he barks at kids running, enlist the neighborhood kids to help you. Have them walk by slowly, reinforcing your dog for not barking. Then have them slowly jog by, then run by, and then maybe even add that ear-piercing scream that most kids know how to do, all while reinforcing your dog for quiet behaviors.

An Almost Surefire Way to Minimize Barking

I know you are going to think I have gone off the deep end with this, but really, it works 99 percent of the time. If your dog is barking at your door or front window, walk up to him, look out, look right and left, and no matter what is (or isn't there), say in a nonchalant voice, "Oh, it's only Uncle Fred" and walk away. Nine times out of ten, your dog will come with you when you leave, so reinforce him for doing so. For some bizarre reason, this *only* works with "Uncle Fred."

My theory (which, I have to admit, I totally made up and have no real notion if it is correct) is this: underling wolves let the wolf in charge know if there is an intruder. Then, the leader wolf, decides whether to ignore, or repel with force. Now, we aren't wolves and neither are our dogs; however, if you let your dog know, "Don't worry, I'll handle it," they usually stop barking.

Yes, I Want You to Bark

Let's say you do want your dog to bark to alert you if someone is coming. (It's not really a bad thing; barking dogs usually repel people who are thinking about breaking and entering.)

Have someone outside who will knock on your cue (use your cell phone to communicate when they should start and stop knocking). They knock, your dog barks, you interrupt after the third bark by clicking and then treat. This is an exercise in timing for you because you only want to allow him three barks. It takes an average of 40 minutes for the dog to figure out that three barks are allowed, and to come and find you after the third one.

Jumping

Say your dog jumps on people who come to the door. Dogs jump to greet people—it is a natural, submissive, greeting behavior and they have to jump because we're taller than they are. Oddly enough (from a human standpoint), the dog thinks that, by offering these submissive behaviors, she's being very polite.

POOCH POINTERS

Contrary to old-fashioned beliefs, jumping up is not a sign of dominance or aggression.

Reactions to Jumping

Half of the people will pet the dog, reinforcing the dog for jumping. You've heard them: "Oh, it's okay; I love dogs." The other half will yank the dog down, squeeze her paws until she is screaming in pain, or knee her in the chest. Or you may yank the dog down or yell at her.

All of these reactions reinforce the dog for jumping—including the negative reactions. Punish the dog for jumping and she may feel the need to jump even more in a submissive, frantic attempt to appease your anger, increasing the cycle of jumping on people. Or the dog may decide that people are dangerous (because so much punishment happens around people) and, as you have learned in previous chapters, the jumping may intensify into fearful biting behaviors or extreme shyness.

Jumping to Solutions

These are some of my favorite options that you can adopt to teach your dog that "four on the floor" is more rewarding for her:

- Avert your eyes and turn sideways as she's about to jump— you can always see the signs in their little eyes or in their bodies! If you miss the signals and the dog jumps, still turn sideways to deflect the dog. Then after she has four on the floor, wait passively for five seconds, ask her to sit, and then reinforce.

- You can also walk away slowly (a calming signal) and reinforce the dog for staying on the ground. Throw treats on the floor to further reinforce that "down there" is better. Play the "Rev Up and Cool Down" game discussed later in this chapter.

- Become a tree stump. Don't move. After all, how reinforcing can a tree stump be? Don't look at the dog, don't talk to the dog, and don't push her away. Trees don't have eyes, ears, mouths, or arms. Just stand there. She'll eventually get down. Wait for five seconds, ask her to sit, and then reinforce.

- Teach the dog to jump on cue by encouraging her to jump and saying, "Up," when she does. Give her a quick pet and murmur, "Good." Then look away and become a stump. *When* you feel the dog get off, say, "Off," and have a party! Give her the jackpot of her life—tons of food, calm petting, praise, and lots of attention. Repeat a billion times. She'll soon learn that the reward for not jumping is infinitely better than the reward for jumping.

- One of my favorite options is to teach the dog to "go visit." "Go visit" means that, *on your cue only*, the dog goes up to the person you're pointing to and lies down! (Lying down is incompatible with jumping.)

- If your dog jumps wildly on people coming to the door, make the doorbell a cue to go to her crate. Or teach the dog that a person approaching is a cue to sit or lie down, and heavily reinforce it.

If your dog still doesn't react appropriately to the preceding options, try the "excuse me" cue:

1. Ask your dog to stand.

2. Step into him perpendicularly, but be sure *not* to touch him. Just lean into him and he should yield (i.e., move away from your pressure). Click and throw the treat on the floor and repeat 6 to 10 times.

3. When he is yielding, you can name it "excuse me" as he is moving away.

4. Don't step directly into his front or he'll just sit and won't be able to get out of your way.

You can start to say, "Excuse me," the instant you see he is about to jump up. If need be, you can just take one step toward him and he'll check himself. "Excuse me" is also a wonderful cue to use when you're racing to the phone and he gets in your way.

DOGGIE DATA

Mark came in with his five-month-old Boxer, Merlin, and his four-and-a-half-year-old daughter Jean. Merlin was body-slamming Jean to the ground on a daily basis. Within one hour, Merlin stopped knocking Jean over, and it has lasted two years so far. Was it magic?

Nope—I just taught Jean to use head turns, body turns, and walking away slowly to reinforce Merlin for being on the ground. The relationship between the two has improved so much so that now Jean is the main trainer of the dog! If a four-and-a-half-year-old child can do it, so can you!

Fluffy, Can I Have My Arm Back Now?

"Ouch! There he goes again! Stop it. *Stop it. I said stop it!* This dog is driving me crazy!" Sound familiar? Biting, as with jumping, can be inadvertently reinforced by your actions. In fact, the cures for biting are similar to those for jumping.

Dogs bite for many reasons: because they can, because that's how they play with other dogs, because they get a "rise" out of us, and because it's fun.

> **POOCH POINTERS**
>
> When was the last time your dog got together with Muffy from down the street to play Parcheesi? Not in your recent memory? Maybe they do when all the humans are sleeping? I think not. Dogs play by biting, body-slamming, chasing, humping, growling, barking, and knocking over furniture. This is normal dog play behavior. It's not aggression—even if the play is directed at you.

Mouthing

If your dog bites you or mouths you, use the calming signals you learned in Chapters 5 and 6—turn sideways, yawn, move slowly away, or sit or lie down (if possible, without being further mauled).

Watch for any patterns of when the biting or mouthing behaviors start. Is it a certain time of day, are you ignoring the dog, or are you overexciting the dog with too-rough play? Is the dog underexercised, overfed, or bored?

> **POOCH POINTERS**
>
> If your dog bites because you're trying to handle or groom her, review the handling guide in Chapter 8.

If he bites you at a certain time of day or when you are too busy to pay attention to him, you have two options: you can start engaging him in play *before* he starts, or you can completely walk away and ignore him. Put a barrier between you two if necessary, or go into another room and shut the door. You must be silent, however, and you can't be silent when you're in pain, so this should be a good incentive for you to watch your dog and stop the biting behavior before it starts!

If your dog is underexercised and overfed, well, you know what you have to do. Get up off the couch and go outside and have a party. Walking sedately around the block on a six-foot leash is not enough aerobic exercise for the normal dog. He needs running, swimming, chasing toys, hiking, long walks in the woods, and whatever else you can think of that your dog likes.

> **POOCH POINTERS**
>
> When you're feeling lazy after a hard day, repeat after me: "A tired dog is a good dog." I don't know about you, but I really love to see my dogs having such a good time, knowing that I'm able to make those fun things possible. Is that egotistical? Maybe, but my dogs are good dogs! I'll have plenty of time to lie around and watch TV in my next life.

You may be stressing out your dog by playing too rough with him. You get rougher and he doesn't know how to get you to stop, so he bites you. Should you be angry? *No!* You're the one who pushed him too far. If this is happening to you, you have some choices. Stop roughhousing with the dog and use toys instead. Or if you insist on playing with him with your not-puncture-resistant arms and hands, stop the play before your dog gets too aroused or stressed. Then pet him lightly and gently to calm him down completely.

Wounded Caribou

This is also called the "Rev Up and Cool Down" game, and I use it for puppies or adolescent dogs who do a lot of jumping or biting when aroused. This is how it works:

1. Run a few steps. (The dog will chase you because that's what dogs like to do most.)

2. After a few steps—before the dog gets too aroused—stop running and walk really sl-o-o-w-ly, and don't look at the dog at all. Keep moving slowly until the dog also slows down. After a few steps of peace and calm, click and treat the dog.

3. Repeat steps 1 and 2. You'll see the dog slow down sooner each time.

4. You can also throw in some Sits and Downs or any other behavior your dog may already know before you reinforce him.

This game teaches the dog to settle down without jumping or nipping by using the dog's own language—moving slowly and turning away.

Biting the Kids

Does your dog chase and bite kids who are running? Then desensitize him to running kids and teach him to ignore them. Or teach the kids to play the "Rev Up and Cool Down" game with the dog. Or use better judgment and don't let the dog be around the kids when they're acting like screaming banshees.

Perhaps your dog bites your kids for inappropriate petting (on the head and back-of-neck areas). So teach them how to pet the dog so that he doesn't feel threatened (review Chapter 8) *and* teach the dog to accept inappropriate petting.

If you have a youngster toddling around, teach your dog to accept pinching and hair pulling. Pinch, and click and treat for no reaction, then pull, and click and treat for no reaction. Don't start out by yanking the dog off his feet—start out lightly, and gradually build to harder pinches (although not so hard as to bruise him).

Can Dogs Really Have ADD?

Of course, dogs can have attention deficit disorder—if you train them! Let's say you want to train your dog and she ignores you, or she has "selective deafness." You cheerlead and possibly bribe with a treat to try to get the dog's attention. When she finally does come to you, you may play with her or give her a treat. She now ignores you more and more for longer and longer periods of time. What were you really reinforcing? The inattention!

DOGGIE DATA

Fran came in with her Golden Retriever, Dexter, for lessons. Dexter had a really bad case of ADD and would ignore Fran about 99 percent of the time. I put them on a "work for a living" program and the results were astounding. Fran was so pleased with Dexter's newfound focus in just one week that she continued to feed Dexter all of his meals from her hand for "jobs."

Go back to the basics from Chapter 7: eye contact, name, recall word, and praise word recognition.

Hand-feed the dog for two weeks—not for free, but for specific behaviors such as Sits, Downs, eye contact, or anything the dog knows how to do. You can "insist" on eye contact going through doors, in and out of the car, in and out of the crate, and from one location to another. Follow these steps:

1. Wait for 30 seconds for the dog to give you eye contact. If she doesn't give you eye contact (with no verbal prodding from you), she gets a trip back to the crate (with no emotion from you; you should periodically give the dog a treat for going back in the crate—yes, even for "failing").

2. Repeat again and again until you get eye contact within 30 seconds.

3. Next, raise your criteria and now wait for only 25 seconds before sending the dog back to her crate. Repeat again and again until you get eye contact within 25 seconds.

4. Then raise your criteria and lower the amount of time that you wait for eye contact.

5. Keep repeating until you get eye contact within three seconds.

As soon as your dog is looking at you within three seconds, you can start working on whatever behaviors you want. If you lose the dog's attention, wait three seconds to see whether you can get it back (again, no verbal prompting from you). If not, back to the crate she goes.

Most people find that this process takes a few weeks or months—depending on how long they've reinforced the dog's inattention. Don't lower your criteria just because you want to train for a specific amount of time or have some other goal in mind. If you do, you'll shoot yourself in the foot by starting the cycle of inattention again. Attention is the foundation of all training and should never be taken for granted.

Pop Quiz

1. In the past, have you inadvertently reinforced your dog for barking, jumping, and so on?

2. If your dog is biting you, look at yourself—are you stressing her? Is she overfed and underworked? Is anyone in the family playing too rough with her?

3. Have you played the "Rev Up and Cool Down" game? (See the earlier section, "Wounded Caribou.")

The Least You Need to Know

- Every time you yell at your dog, hit him, or punish him in any way for barking, jumping, or biting, you're reinforcing those behaviors.
- If you make an issue of jumping and biting, they will become rock-solid behaviors.
- Concentrate on teaching your dog alternative behaviors and watch him carefully for signs that you are pushing him too hard.
- If you aren't ignoring a bad behavior, then you're reinforcing it.

Add Training into Your Life

Chapter 18

In This Chapter

- Training for fifteen minutes a day
- Stop exercising and the muscle will turn to flab
- Don't miss the easy opportunities to train
- A whole new world

I'm sure you're wondering how the heck you're supposed to train your dog when you work full time, but with a little planning you can do it easily. The charts and tips in this chapter show you the way. Then you get a preview of some of the fun training activities for you and your dog down the road.

Consistent Training and Variable Reinforcements Are the Key

When athletes train, they are consistent and dedicated. They know that if they put off training, they'll lose their skills. Dog training is *not* like riding a bike—your dog *will* forget his new behaviors if they aren't practiced. Give yourself a break and *you* will lose the desire to continue.

Although you have to consistently set aside some quality time every day to train your friend, you should vary the frequency and type of reinforcement given during those sessions. But don't confuse "consistency in training" with being variable and unpredictable in how you reinforce.

An Exercise in Creative Training Sessions

If it's hard for you to be creative in setting up your training sessions, try this: write 5 to 10 or more behaviors on separate slips of paper. Here are some examples of desirable behaviors to use:

- Sit
- Backups (make different slips each for no distractions, mild distractions, and lots of distractions)
- Sit stay (10 and 20 seconds)
- Down
- Loose-leash walking (with no distractions, mild distractions, and lots of distractions)
- Down stay (10 and 20 seconds)
- Shake paw
- Sit politely for petting (by you and by someone else)
- Roll over
- Settle (with and without handling)
- Door etiquette in the house, car, and vet's office
- Come (with no distractions, mild distractions, and lots of distractions)
- Stand
- Stand stay (with and without touching)

Fold up the slips and put them in a hat. Every day, pick three behaviors out of a hat and that's what you work on for that day. At the end of the day, put those slips back into the hat to be used again. You can do the same thing with your list of reinforcers. Pick a few out of the hat and those are how you'll reinforce your dog for that session.

As your dog's skill level goes up, exchange the slips for more diffi-cult behaviors. These don't have to be all that complicated—just pick things that will stimulate his brain. Here are a few examples:

- Hide a treat or toy in a blanket or towel and encourage the dog to find it. This encourages him to use his nose—great for scent-discrimination exercises for more advanced training.

- Show him a toy, tell him to stay, and then hide the toy (in plain sight at first). Then release him to find it. You can gradually make your hiding places harder and harder.

- Teach him to touch his nose to a target—such as your hand or a plastic lid. Nose targeting is great for many things—it teaches the dog to turn his head away from another dog to avoid potential problems (head turning is a calming signal). Targeting a plastic lid is great for when you're teaching some of the obstacles in agility training.

- Get a Kong toy and fill it with gooey things and some hard treats that are slightly bigger than the opening. This will give him a little mental puzzle to keep him happy and busy.

There are many simple ways to add enrichment and variability to your dog's life without going too crazy. You can even teach him service-dog behaviors, such as picking up keys—or better yet—*finding* keys, closing cabinet doors (I wouldn't recommend teaching him to open cabinet doors), or retrieving your slippers. I recently taught Emma to retrieve the phone for me in case of an emergency. She is so proud of herself, as she should be! Sidenote: I did not teach all of my dogs to do this because I didn't want them fighting over the phone when it counts.

Training Goals

No one is ever done with training, but there are some behaviors you should strive for, as recommended by noted positive trainer Ted Turner. Teach all of these and you will be the envy of every other dog owner you meet!

- Eye contact
- Name recognition
- Praise-word recognition
- Walking on a loose leash
- Walking on a loose leash with attention to you
- Accepting petting, handling, and grooming
- Stays (with distractions)
- Recall (with distractions)
- Crate training
- Control in and out of doorways and cars
- Potty training
- Allowing food removal and ignoring dropped food
- No aggression to humans or dogs
- No jumping, mouthing, or biting
- Tolerance of children
- Not totally reliant on food as a reinforcer

Please don't think that these are unattainable—they aren't. It just takes consistency, patience, specific goals on your part, and faith that your dog—yes, *your* dog—can achieve this level of training.

Incorporating Training into Your Routine

I know it's hard sometimes to think about training your dog when you come home tired, but you owe it to yourself and to your dog. After all, why else did you get a dog if not to have fun with her? After you just do it, you should find that your energy level actually increases and your mental state improves. It has been proven that when hospital or nursing-home patients are around dogs, they're happier and more relaxed.

> **CANINE CAVEATS**
>
> When running errands while training your dog, be sure to watch the weather. In even relatively mild weather (65 degrees and higher), a dog can die of heatstroke in six minutes if left in a closed and unprotected car. Even if he doesn't die, he can suffer irreparable brain damage.

You can train your dog almost any time of day or night—while you cook, eat, clean, talk on the phone, work on the computer, watch TV, run errands, go to a softball game, go swimming, take a hike, or ride a bike.

A typical day of running errands and training at the same time can be the following:

- Go to the bank, bring the dog with you, and practice door etiquette.

- Pick up your dry cleaning and practice loose-leash walking in the parking lot.

- While doing your laundry at the Laundromat, practice stays and eye contact, and play the "hide the cookie" or "toy in the towel" game. You can even put the dog on a longer leash and practice recalls.

- When you go to the pet shop, practice door etiquette, sitting politely for petting, and loose-leash walking.

So you see, it's not hard to find time to work with your dog. My hope for you is that you become a training junkie and sell your couch and TV to make room for training equipment!

An Apple a Day

If you spend as little as three five-minute sessions per day training your dog, you'll have a good dog. The sessions don't have to be strictly formal—you can train your dog while running errands or doing chores around the house. You can (and should) train while you play with her and play while you train. Your dog should not know the difference between playing and training—both should be equally fun and satisfying. What may actually happen is that you end up enjoying the sessions because your dog soaks up whatever you teach her. You'll see positive results and that will spur you on to train more.

DOGGIE DATA

Bobbi grumbled about one of the charts that showed how to train while cleaning. Her complaint? "But that means I have to clean!"

Following the training charts in this section will ...

- Keep you on track with each new behavior.

- Advance each behavior in small approximations (steps).

- Help you become variable in how you reinforce.

- Give you an idea of how you can train your dog, even while cleaning the house.

Sample Training Guides

These charts are a checklist and guideline for training. They list the many different behaviors you can work on, plus how you can be variable and unpredictable in how you reinforce each repetition. After you get the hang of this, you can make up your own charts based on the behaviors your dog still needs to learn.

WEEK ONE

Monday

Sit
— 2 treats
— 5 treats
— pets & praise
— 1 treat & pet
— ball toss

Backups
— 10 treats
— 1 treat
— ball toss
— 4 treats
— pets & praise
— 6 treats

Eye Contact
— 1 treat
— 4 treats
— pets & praise
— 1 treat
— run away silly
— 4 treats

Come, click & treat
For 5 minutes

Sit
— 2 treats
— 3 treats
— pet & 1 treat
— praise
— 5 treats

Eye Contact
— 1 treat
— 2 treats
— ball toss
— praise
— petting
— 5 treats

Tuesday

Down
— 10 treats
— pet and 2 treats
— ball toss
— 1 treat
— 4 treats

Eye contact
— pets & praise
— 3 treats
— 1 treat
— pet & ball toss
— 1 treat
— 1 treat

Sit
— praise
— 1 treat
— ball toss
— run away silly
— 4 treats
— run away silly
— 4 treats

Backups
— 1 treat
— 1 treat
— 6 treats
— run away silly
— 2 treats
— pets & praise

Come, click & treat
for 2 minutes

Down
— 5 treats
— 2 treats
— pets & praise
— pets & 8 treats
— pets and water

Wednesday

Eye contact
— 1 treat
— 2 treats
— pets & praise
— pet & 1 treat
— 1 treat

Name, click, treat
For 5 minutes

Cuddle time

Down
— 9 treats
— ball toss
— 3 treats
— run away silly

Sit
— praise
— Praise and pets
— 4 treats
— 1 treat

Sit before you
throw the toy.

Down before you
throw the toy.

Name, click & treat
for 5 minutes

Backups
— 1 treat
— 4 treats

Thursday

Cuddle time

Come, click & treat
For 5 minutes

Name, click & treat
for 5 minutes

Sit for toy tosses

Down for toy tosses

Eye contact for
toy tosses

Stand
— 1 treat
— 2 treats
— 1 treat
— 5 treats

Cuddle time

Eye contact for petting

Sit
— 1 treat
— hand clapping
— run away silly
— ball toss
— 4 treats

Friday

Stand
— 3 treats
— gentle petting
— 1 treat
— 5 treats

Eye contact, click & treat
for 3 minutes

Put leash on, click
and treat. Then take
leash off, click and
treat – repeat 10 times

Backups
— 4 treats
— petting
— Praise
— 7 treats
— 1 treat

Hide & Seek – praise,
treats and petting
— in the bathroom
— in the bedroom
— in the closet
— in the kitchen

Touch top of head
game – repeat 10 times,
clicking & treating for
no movement away

Cuddle time

Saturday

Go to a field
and play with dog
on a 50-foot long line

While playing, add in:

Eye contact, click
& treat for 2 minutes

Name, click &
treat for 3 minutes

3 sits
— 3 treats
— petting
— 1 treat

4 downs
— petting
— praise
— 5 treats

Backups
— 6 treats
— praise
— 1 treat
— ball toss

Once at home,
Put leash on, click
and treat. Then take
leash off, click and
treat – repeat 10 times

Touch top of head and
neck areas – repeat 10
times, clicking & treating
for no movement away.

Week 1 training guide.

WEEK TWO

Monday

Sit
___ 1 treats
___ 7 treats
___ pets & praise
___ 1 treat & pet
___ ball toss

Stand stay
___ 1 second
___ 2 seconds
___ 3 seconds
___ 4 seconds
___ 5 seconds
___ 6 seconds

Eye Contact
___ 1 treat
___ 1 treat
___ pets & praise
___ 2 treats
___ 1 treat
___ run away silly
___ 4 treats

Come, click & treat
For 5 minutes

Stand w/touching
___ 1 treats
___ 2 treats
___ pet & 1 treat
___ praise
___ 5 treats

Name, click & treat
for 3 minutes

Tuesday

Down
___ 10 treats
___ pet and 2 treats
___ ball toss
___ 1 treat
___ 4 treats

"Shamu" Down stay
___ 3 seconds
___ 3 seconds
play for 4 minutes

"Shamu" Down stay
___ 3 seconds
___ 4 seconds
___ 4 seconds

Sit
___ praise
___ 1 treat
___ ball toss
___ run away silly
___ 4 treats
___ pet & 3 treats
___ pet

Backups w/distractions
___ 4 treats
___ 2 treat
___ 6 treats
___ run away silly
___ 2 treats
___ pets & praise

Come, click & treat
or 2 minutes

Wednesday

Throw the cookie game
___ 10 treats
___ 12 treats
___ pets & praise
___ pet & 1 treat
___ 7 treats

"Shamu" down stay
___ 4 seconds
___ 6 seconds
___ 6 seconds

Name, click, treat
For 5 minutes

Stand for touching
___ 4 treats
___ 3 treats
___ 5 treats

Sit for toy tosses

Eye contact for toy tosses

Sit
___ praise
___ Praise and pets
___ 4 treats
___ 1 treat
___ run away silly

Practice door etiquette

Practice food bowl etiquette

Name, click & treat
for 5 minutes

Thursday

Eye contact
___ 1 treat
___ petting
___ praise
___ 8 treats

Come, click & treat
For 5 minutes

Throw the cookie game
___ 6 treats
___ 8 treats
___ 10 treats
___ petting & 11 treats

Cuddle time

"Shamu" Down stay
___ 6 seconds
___ 10 seconds
___ 10 seconds

Eye contact for toy tosses

Stand stay
___ 1 treat
___ 2 treats
___ 1 treat
___ 5 treats

Cuddle time

Eye contact for petting

**Put leash on, click
and treat. Then take
leash off, click and
treat – repeat 10 times**

Friday

"Shamu" down stays
___ 10 seconds
___ 18 seconds
___ 18 seconds

**Eye contact, click &
treat for 3 minutes**

**Put leash on, click
and treat. Then take
leash off, click and
treat – repeat 10 times**

Backups w/ distractions
___ 4 treats
___ petting
___ run away silly
___ 7 treats
___ 1 treat

**Hide & Seek – praise,
treats and petting**
___ in the bathroom
___ in the bedroom
___ in the closet
___ in the kitchen

**Touch top of head game
– repeat 10 times, clicking
& treating for no
movement away**

Cuddle time

**Play fetch for eye contact,
sits and downs**

Saturday

**Go to a field and
play with dog on a
50-foot long line**

While playing, add in:

**The two toy game
and the two tug game.
Be sure to play by
your rules.**

**Name, click & treat
for 3 minutes**

**Backups or perhaps
loose leash walking
if your dog is focused
on you.**

**Teach your dog
how to shake paw**

"Shamu" down stays
___ 18 seconds
___ 34 seconds
___ 34 seconds

**Once at home,
Put leash on, click
and treat. Then take
leash off, click and
treat – repeat 10 times**

Cuddle time

Week 2 training guide.

WEEK THREE

Monday

Drop the cookie game
___ 1 treat
___ 7 treats
___ pets & praise
___ 2 tug games
___ 4 treats

Loose-leash walking
___ 1 step (C/T)
___ 1 step (C/T)
___ 1 step (C/T)
___ 1 step (C/T)
___ 1 step (C/T)

"Shamu" down stays
___ 34 seconds
___ 34 seconds
___ 66 seconds

Practice "Shake paw"

Cuddle time

Name, click & treat for 3 minutes

Food bowl etiquette

Water bowl etiquette

Sit
___ 4 treats
___ 1 treat
___ petting
___ praise

Tuesday

Door etiquette
___ front door
___ back door
___ side door

"Shamu" Down stay
___ 66 seconds

___ play for 5 minutes

Stand stay for petting
___ head
___ shoulder
___ back
___ head

Sit
___ praise
___ 1 treat
___ ball toss
___ run away silly
___ 4 treats
___ pet & 3 treats
___ pet

Loose-leash walking
___ 1 step (C/T)
___ 2 steps (C/T)
___ 2 steps (C/T)
___ 2 steps (C/T)
___ 2 steps (C/T)
___ 2 steps (C/T)

Have someone hold your dog's leash, while you call the dog. Make sure they drop the leash as soon as you say "come." As reinforcers, use food, petting, praise, runaway silly, and toys

Wednesday

Real Life
___ 2 toy game while dusting
___ down stay while doing dishes
___ down stay
___ while vacuuming
___ throw the cookie game while working on computer

Loose leash walking
___ 3 steps (C/T)
___ 3 steps (C/T)
___ 3 steps (C/T)
___ 3 steps (C/T)
___ 3 steps (C/T)

Name, click, treat For 5 minutes

Door etiquette
___ in the car
___ coming out of car
___ at the bank
___ at the post office
___ at the Laundromat

Cuddle time

Teach your dog to "wave" Bonus points if you teach the dog to shake and wave with both paws!

Settle
___ 5 treats
___ 3 treats
___ 4 treats
___ 1 treat
___ run away silly

Thursday

Settle
___ 1 treat
___ light petting
___ 3 treats
___ 6 treats

Name, click & treat For 5 minutes

Drop the cookie game
___ petting
___ praise & 8 treats
___ 6 treats
___ petting & 3 treats

Settle with a stay
___ 9 treats
___ 3 treats
___ 1 treat
___ light petting
___ 5 treats

"Shamu" Down stay
___ 66 seconds
___ 66 seconds

Sits for toy tosses

Stand stay
___ for paw touches
___ for head touch
___ for leaning over in an obnoxious way

Eye contact for petting & toy toss

Put leash on, click and treat. Then take leash off, click and treat – repeat 10 times

Friday

Teach your dog to roll over

Name, click & treat for 3 minutes

Stand stay
___ for head touch
___ for tail touch
___ for paw touch

Loose leash walking
___ 4 steps (C/T)
___ 5 steps (C/T)
___ 5 steps (C/T)
___ 5 steps (C/T)
___ 5 steps (C/T)

2 tug game – don't forget the rules! Add in a sit or down before allowing the dog to retake the toy.

"Shamu" sit stays
___ 3 seconds
___ 3 seconds
___ 3 seconds

Cuddle time

Sit still while you brush for treats. Keep it slow – 1 brush stroke at a time. Continue in this vein, adding more and more brushing. Have someone help you by feeding it dog is still.

Saturday

Show off to your friends all you have taught your dog in ONLY 3 weeks! Congratulations!!!

Loose leash walking for 5 steps

Sit

Down

Down stay for 66 seconds

Stand & stay for handling

Shake paw and wave

Settle

Roll over

Name recognition

Come word recognition

Door etiquette

Staying still for petting

Not leaving you even if the leash is off, until you release the dog

Fetch games for eye contact, sits and downs

Week 3 training guide.

As you can see, this is all pretty basic stuff that will fit easily into your busy schedule. You'll notice that, in the beginning, lots of food is used, but as the weeks go on, other types of reinforcers are used to keep the behaviors intact.

Where All This Fun Might Lead You

Okay, so now you're completely and utterly hooked on dog training. Your dog is performing incredible behaviors and you want *more!* Good for you—and great for your dog! Never fear, there are plenty of additional activities you can do with your dog.

Therapy Dog

Most hospitals, nursing homes, and schools welcome therapy dogs. The primary objective for a therapy dog is to provide comfort and companionship to patients. The dogs increase emotional well-being, promote healing, and improve the quality of life for the people they visit.

> **DOGGIE DATA**
>
> Many years ago, I took my Sheltie, Noel, to a nursing home. One time, a nurse asked me if I could put Noel in bed with a woman who had been comatose for many years. When I did, the nurse took the woman's hand and had her gently pet Noel. Within seconds there was a definite positive reaction from the patient.

For your dog to be a registered therapy dog, he must first pass his Canine Good Citizen (CGC) test (see Chapter 19), as well as be trained to ignore dropped food (not really as hard as you may think!) and be calm around wheelchairs, walkers, and canes. In addition, the dog needs to be relaxed around people walking erratically and be willing to be handled by strangers and to actively seek out petting. Your dog must be at least one year old to take the test.

There are many organizations that you can register with to enable your dog to become a therapy dog. They generally offer insurance (in case your dog accidentally hurts someone) that is usually inexpensive. The Delta Society and Therapy Dog International are the two largest organizations. If your dog is not registered with a group, you will not be allowed to enter hospitals or nursing homes with him.

Rally-O

This is a new sport that's a natural stepping-stone from the CGC to competition obedience or agility (see the following sections for more on these dog sports). Many of the maneuvers are similar to competition obedience, but you can talk to your dog the entire time while giving extra cues. You follow a course of signs and do the behaviors listed on the signs, rather than responding to a judge's commands as you would in competition obedience.

Rally-O is a great way to acclimate you and your dog to the "show scene" in a fun, exciting, and nonscary way. The scoring is less stringent than competition obedience and is great for the trainer who isn't quite sure what he or she wants to do next. Train for Rally-O and you can go on to competition obedience or agility with ease.

The Association of Pet Dog Trainers (APDT) offers titles in Rally for all breeds and mixed breeds, and the American Kennel Club (AKC) and ASCA (Australian Shepherd Club of America) now offers Rally as a titling event.

Competition Obedience

Competition obedience is the foundation upon which all other dog sports are based. Training for competition develops a strong working relationship between the dog and her owner. A few of the behaviors your dog must master to earn the three main titles are heeling on- and off-leash at different paces, standing still while a stranger lightly examines the dog, "sit stays" and "down stays" in a group of other dogs, dumbbell retrieves, jumping, and scent discrimination.

There are three main levels of obedience competition: Novice, Open, and Utility. You can also train for and earn an Obedience Trial Champion (OTCH) title. The levels increase in complexity and really hone your skills as a trainer. Any one of the titles says a great deal about you and your dog, your relationship, and your dedication. Your dog can wear these titles proudly!

Three main registries promote competition obedience. The AKC allows only purebred dogs to compete in its trials. The United Kennel Club (UKC) allows mixed-breed dogs to enter, and the Australian Shepherd Club of America (ASCA) allows any breed as well as mixed breeds to compete in its trials. The American Mixed Breed Obedience Registry (AMBOR) is only for mixed breeds.

Agility

Very simply, agility is an obstacle course for dogs. Your dog must follow the course correctly, accurately, safely, and *quickly!* There are many levels and types of classes offered that will fit into most people's and dog's abilities.

Agility is fun and challenging for both dog and handler. The AKC offers agility trials (purebred dogs only) as do the North American Agility Council (NADAC) and United States Dog Agility Association (USDAA). These last two registries allow purebred and mixed-breed dogs to compete.

Many people may think competition obedience or Rally is too hard and may want to skip right to agility. Granted, agility may seem like more fun, but you really can't do agility without basic obedience. After all, your dog will be off-leash while other dogs and people are outside the ring, and you will need to know that your dog will stay with you. So although you can do competition obedience without agility, you can't do agility without obedience!

Sheep Herding

You can train for sheep herding with just about any breed of dog that has any "sheep sense." I've even seen Standard Poodles and German

Shorthaired Pointers do a fine job herding sheep. However, if you want to actually compete, you can do so only with a breed of dog that the AKC classifies as part of the Herding group (for example, Border Collies, Old English Sheepdogs, and Corgis). The AKC and ASCA are the two registries that hold herding trials. There are also many trials for Border Collies only.

Musical Freestyle

Musical freestyle is "dancing with your dog" to music. Many of the behaviors you can use are fun and funny. The great thing about freestyle is that the only limitations are your own imagination. If you like music, have even a slight sense of rhythm (I don't, but I still like to train the behaviors), and like to be creative, then freestyle is for you. Many people aren't interested in competing for titles, but use their routines for demos at pet fairs or at nursing homes, or at the very least to amaze and impress their friends. You don't need any special equipment and it's great to practice on those rainy days. World Canine Freestyle Organization (WCFO) even offers the ability to compete for titles via videotape.

Other Sports

There are additional dog sports for many other breeds, such as tracking, search and rescue, carting (pulling a cart), weight pull, flyball (a timed relay race, with a team of four dogs jumping over four hurdles, taking a tennis ball out of a "flyball box," and jumping back over the four hurdles), earthdog (or "go to ground," where terriers find the rodents who are caged underground), canine water sports (all breeds and mixed), lure coursing (chasing a "lure" through a prescribed course), conformation (a beauty contest for purebred dogs—think "Westminster Kennel Club dog show"), and water rescue. For more information, see Appendix B. Each of these sports has a personality of its own. You will meet some wonderful people and develop great new friendships that will change your life—and your dog's life—for the better.

Pop Quiz

1. How many places have you taken your dog to train?

2. Have you been able to train your dog for at least three five-minute sessions per day?

3. Have you been diligent about using reinforcers other than food?

4. Have you thought about what dog sport you'd like to learn more about?

The Least You Need to Know

- Train a few minutes every day and you will have a great dog.
- Use the places on your daily errand list as opportunities to train your dog.
- Lay down your dog's foundation behaviors and the sky's the limit for what you can accomplish.
- Get involved with some dog sports and make new friends.

The Canine Good Citizen Test

In This Chapter

- Proper greetings
- I am a loose-leash-walkin' fool!
- Nothing fazes me
- I "vont" to be alone

Using positive methods, you've taught your dog all the essentials she'll need to pass the Canine Good Citizen (CGC) test. The purpose of the CGC is to ensure that your best friend will be invited back as a welcome guest wherever she goes. Earning your CGC title says a great deal about you and your dog. It says that you took the time and effort to properly teach your dog the much-needed skills to be a respected member of society and, in some instances, to enable you to get or even keep your homeowner's insurance. It also says that you took training seriously and that you understand the importance of a formal education for your four-footed friend. In short, it speaks a lot for you, too.

Nice to Meet Ya!

Ten sections make up the CGC test. The first three are accepting a friendly stranger, sitting politely for petting, and appearance and grooming. The following sections explore what you'll need to practice for each part of the test.

Accepting a Friendly Stranger

Your dog is to be at your side, preferably sitting or lying down. The tester approaches and the dog should remain in position, or, at the very least, should not maul the tester. The tester shakes hands with you and does not interact with your dog. You may talk to your dog, and remind him to stay.

The best way to teach this is to teach your dog that a person approaching is a cue to sit. This is very easy to teach and can be done in six steps:

1. Hold the dog on the leash. Be sure not to pull on the dog if he starts to jump. Just be a rock.

2. Have a person approach and have that person ask the dog to sit. (You can show the person your hand signal for "sit.")

POOCH POINTERS

If you've done a lot of work with your dog in front of you, you now need to teach her to be comfortable at your side. Just have her sit next to you and feed her for being in that position. After a few minutes of getting fed there, she will stop whirling around in front of you.

3. After the dog sits, the person who approached your dog can give him a treat after you click for the sit.

4. Repeat bunches of times (usually after five to six times the dog sits automatically). You may also want to build up some duration between the sit and the treat so that your dog doesn't expect a treat within one second and then get annoyed if that person doesn't deliver (remember scheduled-induced aggression from Chapter 3?).

5. When the dog sits automatically, the person no longer has to say the word "sit," although you may still want to say it yourself.

6. Now change your stranger to a new person and repeat all the preceding steps.

The more you do this with new people, the faster your dog will generalize. Be sure, however, that you do *not* yank on the leash if the dog does jump. Just have the person stay out of leash range at first and wait for your dog to get down. Remind him to sit and have the person approach again.

A dog accepting a friendly stranger.
(Photo by P. Dennison)

Sitting Politely for Petting

This exercise is almost the same as the first one. The idea is to get the dog used to people petting him without getting upset or jumping. The tester will approach your dog. The dog should be in either a "sit" or a "down." The tester then lightly pets your dog.

After your dog has learned the first step, training for this one is a piece of cake. Follow these steps:

1. Have the stranger approach your dog while you remind your dog to sit.

2. As the stranger reaches out to pet your dog, feed your dog a treat. As soon as the petting stops, stop feeding the treats.

3. Have the person walk away and then walk back and do it again.

4. After about five to six times, you shouldn't need to feed your dog because he is now comfortable with a stranger petting him.

5. Change your stranger to a new person and repeat all the preceding steps.

If at any time your dog jumps, don't yank him down. Don't forget that the opposition reflex causes the dog to push or pull against anything that is pushing or pulling against him. The more you yank on your dog, the more he will jump.

Appearance and Grooming

This test shows that your dog will accept handling from a stranger such as a groomer or veterinarian. The tester approaches your dog, lightly brushes him (just a few strokes), lifts up and examines each front foot, and touches each ear.

When training, break this exercise into three parts: brushing, foot lifting, and then ear touching. Here's what to do:

CANINE CAVEATS

Make sure your dog is comfortable with you doing these things before having your stranger do them. Review Chapter 8 to make sure that your dog is perfectly relaxed about being handled in this way.

Taking the last set of steps, you can now add in brushing along with the touching of each body part. Remember to go slow so as not to distress your dog.

When your dog is comfortable with strangers brushing him, repeat all the preceding steps but insert paw lifting after the brushing. After he's doing well with his feet being touched, you can add ear touches.

Accepting ear touches.
(Photo by P. Dennison)

If you practice these three sections religiously, your dog will breeze through them come test time.

POOCH POINTERS

The obvious benefit to these exercises is that your dog will welcome petting and handling by strangers and not need to be muzzled for grooming and vet visits.

Accepting paw touches.
(Photo by P. Dennison)

Walking and Chewing Gum

Sections 4 and 5 of the test have to do with loose-leash walking. Review Chapter 10 and make sure you've taken it "on the road" and proofed loose-leash walking in all kinds of strange places before you take the test.

The dog doesn't have to be in rigid "heel" position, because this is not competition obedience. The tester just needs to see that the dog is attentive to you and will stay with you if you change direction. You'll be directed to lead your dog in a right turn, a left turn, and an about turn (a 180-degree turnaround), with a stop in between and one at the end. Don't forget that you can talk to your dog and encourage him to follow you as you make each turn.

Out for a Walk

Section 4, "out for a walk," demonstrates that you can walk your dog on a loose leash and that *she* doesn't walk *you*. She may be on either your right or left side, whichever you prefer. The dog doesn't need to sit when you stop, but it helps in keeping her attention.

If the leash is pulled tight continually or the dog sniffs the ground excessively, the dog will not pass the test. Be sure to practice using the other types of reinforcers listed in Chapter 8, because food is not allowed during the CGC test.

CANINE CAVEATS

Practice in many locations. Sometimes the tests are held indoors and sometimes outdoors. Some dogs do better inside without the distractions of nature, and some dogs do better outside without the "pressure" of a small building or room. Train for both and you won't have to worry.

Walking Through a Crowd

This test for Section 5 shows that your dog can walk politely in a crowd of people without jumping on them or ripping your shoulder out of its socket. Your dog can show some interest in the crowd, but must continue to walk with you. Sniffing a person briefly is allowed, but the dog should come back to you and proceed with your walk.

Because you've done your homework, this should be pretty easy for you and your dog. If you're still having problems with this, don't despair. Just practice more, continuing to make it fun for your dog to ignore people. Heavily reinforce with petting, food, and toys when he leaves strangers alone.

If you have to, stay far away from groups of people and gradually move in closer and closer. The nearer you are to the group, the more heavily you should reinforce his attention. After a while, you should be able to wean him off of the bigger reinforcers and just use praise and petting.

DOGGIE DATA

Food and toys are not allowed during the CGC test, but petting and praise are. Make sure you've built up longer behavior patterns *and* have built up the value of verbal praise and petting.

Walking through a crowd.
(Photo by P. Dennison)

Here, There, and Everywhere

Sections 6 and 7 show that the dog has training and will respond to your cues of "sit," "down," and "stay." Because you've practiced this in many different contexts, this will be a walk in the park for you.

Sit, Down, and Staying in Place

The tester will ask you to have your dog do a "sit" or "down." As you already learned, you don't need to push or pull the dog into position, and these methods are not allowed during the test anyway.

Prior to this test, a 20-foot lead is attached to the dog's collar. After the dog does the "sit" and "down," you will be instructed to ask the dog to "stay." You can do either a "sit stay" or a "down stay"— whichever your dog does better. Then walk out to the end of the 20-foot line, turn around, and come right back. You can say, "Stay,

stay, stay," the entire time. You won't need to if you've trained properly, but if it makes you feel better, you can repeat the cues.

> **POOCH POINTERS**
>
> You can talk to your dog incessantly throughout the test. In fact, I recom-
> mend talking to your dog to relax both of you.

Coming When Called

This test demonstrates that the dog will come when called. While
the dog is still on the 20-foot line, you will walk 10 feet away from
her, telling her to "wait" or "stay." Then you call your dog to you.
You can use thigh slapping or verbal encouragement and can call
the dog numerous times. However, you won't have to because you've
trained her to respond on the first cue!

Solid as a Rock

Sections 8 and 9 show that your dog won't have a fearful or aggressive reaction to distractions or other dogs. A Good Citizen is not just
about being good around human strangers, but around dog strangers
as well.

Reaction to Distractions

There are two types of distractions used during Section 8: a visual
one and an audible one. The tester might use a person on crutches,
a walker, or a wheelchair; the sudden opening or closing of a door;
a jogger or bicyclist; a person pushing a shopping cart; or someone
clanging metal bowls or dropping a large book.

To train for these things, start with the audible distractions. Set up
your sessions carefully, and gradually make the distractions bigger.
Here's what you should do:

1. Start with a small paperback book and drop it on the floor
    while feeding the dog simultaneously.

2. Repeat a few times to ensure that the dog has no reaction.

3. Graduate to a larger book and repeat steps 1 and 2.

Provided that the dog didn't react to the books, you can now add something a little noisier, such as a metal bowl or pan. Continue to feed him simultaneously while dropping the objects.

CANINE CAVEATS

Your dog is permitted to show a casual interest in the noise or sight distractions, but she can't show fear, resentment, or shyness. She can even startle slightly, but must not try to pull away in fear. She also has to show that she can recover from the startle within a short period of time and not remain shaking or cowering.

Obviously, urinating or defecating in fear, or barking and lunging, are not acceptable. A few barks may be all right if the dog is then silent.

Persevere in training using more and louder noises, always making sure that you feed your dog for calm behaviors. If at any time your dog shows nervousness or fear, move back a step and reinforce at the last level he was successful. Then move up the ladder at a slower rate.

Now you can add visual distractions. Start back at the beginning, using a mild one, such as a kid's wheelbarrow or even someone walking a bicycle. As you did with audible distractions, add bigger items that are moving faster and faster.

POOCH POINTERS

As the distraction passes by, you're allowed to remind your dog to stay. Don't underestimate the power of "stay." If a dog is slightly nervous, responding to a cue from you may just help him relax; it gives him a job to do.

Reaction to Another Dog

Passing Section 9 is another sure sign that you've done a fantastic job training your dog. Another handler and neutral dog will approach you and your dog. When you're within arm's length of each other, you will all stop and ask your dog to sit or lie down.

You and the other handler will shake hands and exchange pleasantries for a few seconds and then move away from each other. The dogs will be on the outside (left) of the handlers as they approach each other. Your dog can show a mild interest in the other dog, but must show no fear, shyness, aggression, panic, or "Hi there, let's dump these humans and go play!"

> **DOGGIE DATA**
>
> If the distraction dog creates a ruckus, you can ask to take that portion of the test again with a more appropriate dog. You are entitled to a "neutral" dog.

You can teach your dog to accept a neutral dog the same way you taught her to accept a friendly stranger. Take it in small steps, heavily reinforcing your dog for remaining calm around the other dog. I like to start with two dogs, walking far apart and parallel to each other (walking parallel is a calming signal). When your dog is comfortable, gradually come in a little closer. When you are walking almost side by side, you can start walking toward each other. Start out far away and gradually come in closer and closer.

Two dogs walking parallel to each other with handlers in between.
(Photo by P. Dennison)

Two dogs and their handlers approaching, stopping and shaking hands. Both dogs are quite at ease next to their handlers.

(Photo by P. Dennison)

So Long, Farewell

Supervised separation is the last and sometimes the hardest section of the CGC test. This test shows that your dog can be left alone for three minutes with a stranger and maintain his good manners and training. The dog doesn't have to stay in position, but isn't allowed to jump on the evaluator or otherwise be a pest. The dog also is not permitted to whine, bark, howl, growl, pace, or show anything more than mild agitation.

Training for supervised separation need not be traumatic for your dog. Just as with everything else in positive training, break it down into tiny approximations and you'll have a dog who doesn't freak out if you leave him.

> **CANINE CAVEATS**
>
> If the test is held outside, urinating or defecating is allowed for only this test. If, however, the test is held indoors, either action is an immediate cause for failure.

> **DOGGIE DATA**
>
> This seemingly useless test is actually a fantastic experience for your dog. You don't like to think about it, but what would happen to your dog if something happened to you? Would he be able to move nicely and serenely into a new home, or would he freak out at being away from you?
>
> Although having a great relationship with your dog is essential, you also want your dog to be able to be with other people. At the very least, I'm sure you'd like to go on vacation without your dog being traumatized.

To train for supervised separation, follow these steps:

1. Start out with a friend whom the dog knows and likes.

2. Go out of sight for three seconds. Have your friend feed the dog a few treats while you're gone.

3. When you come back, don't go crazy with praise; soft petting and praise are sufficient.

4. Leave again for five seconds while your friend feeds the dog.

Be sure to use a timer when you practice this so that you don't inadvertently leave for too long. Continue adding a few seconds more each time until you gradually build up to three minutes of your dog being calm without you.

Your friend should also start feeding less after you've reached the full three minutes. If at any time your dog gets nervous, have your friend try to redirect to simple behaviors such as a "sit" or "down." He or she can also try some of the calming signals such as yawning or lip licking. Be sure that the friend doesn't inadvertently reinforce your dog for being nervous by talking, petting, or comforting her.

Above all, do not rush this. If your dog gets too nervous, you don't want to come back to her, because then she learns that her nervousness brings you back. You want her to learn that her *calmness* is what brings you back.

Keep your comings and goings low-key. Although it's good for your ego when your dog goes ballistic in greeting you (even if you leave for only five seconds), it's not healthy for the dog. Practice building for a few extra minutes more than you'll need. Most competition trainers teach their dogs to do the stay exercises for longer than needed. For instance, they will train a two-minute "sit stay" rather than the one minute needed in the ring. Why? Because when they are really competing, it will be easier for the dog.

Practice these exercises in many locations and you'll ace your test. I also recommend that you watch a CGC test without your dog along, so that you know what to expect when she's ready. You'll learn the flow of the tests and how they're handled, and it will help keep your stress level low. Prepare yourself, prepare your dog, and then pick out a beautiful new frame and prominent location to hang your Canine Good Citizen certificate! Congratulations!

The Least You Need to Know

- Put together the behaviors you taught your dog in previous chapters to train your dog to earn his CGC title.
- Teach your dog to ignore and accept friendly strangers, other dogs, and handling.
- The basic manners of "sit," "down," "stay," and loose-leash walking will take you far.
- Teach your dog to be comfortable being away from you for even longer periods of time than needed for the test.

Glossary

adrenaline and **glucocorticoids**   Hormones that are produced in mammals during stress to help the body prepare for a fight-or-flight response.

alpha   The dog in charge. Very often people misinterpret which dog is alpha, incorrectly thinking that the bully or the most aggressive dog is the "alpha" dog.

alpha roll   Grappling a dog to the ground and holding him in a submissive position.

antecedent   A cue, or something that comes before a behavior.

approximations   Small steps that make up a final behavior.

arcing   A behavior that dogs exhibit when they meet. Rather than going straight up to each other, they walk around in a big circle, at times even curving their bodies.

behavior   What the animal does, resulting from a cue.

behavior extinction   Withholding all reinforcement for a given behavioral response. This will reduce the frequency of the response.

CERF   Canine Eye Registry Foundation. A centralized national registry of dogs who have been certified free of inheritable eye diseases.

consequence   What happens directly after a behavior.

continuous schedule of reinforcement   Giving your dog a treat each and every time she does a correct behavior.

counterconditioning   The use of associative learning to reverse the unwanted effects of prior conditioning.

criteria   What behaviors you will accept from your dog during a particular training session.

desensitization or **systematic desensitization**   A form of counterconditioning; a procedure in which a phobic (scared) subject (human or animal) is subjected to low levels of the frightening stimulus while relaxed. The level of frightening stimulus is gradually increased, but never at a rate to cause distress. Eventually the fear dissipates.

dominant   Assertive or pushy, not aggressive. Some dogs (as well as some people) don't know how to take no for an answer and will continue to push and push. Many pushy dogs are labeled dominant, but there are many definitions of this term and most of them are negative.

glucocorticoids   *See* adrenaline.

hackles   The hair along a dog's spine or neck. A dog's hackles will rise up when she's nervous.

hips and elbows   A dog's hips and elbows need to be checked and certified as sound before he can be bred. If a dog with a history of hip dysplasia or elbow problems is bred, the health problems will be passed along to future generations, causing heartache and pain to the dogs and their humans.

jackpot   Giving the dog lots of treats, one at a time. I like to give a jackpot when the dog has done something hard for the very first time or if a behavior is particularly wonderful.

learned helplessness   When the dog (or human) shuts down because nothing he does is ever right. The dog just gives up.

lumping   When you try to train huge portions of a behavior all at the same time; for instance, trying to get a dog to walk on a loose leash for a mile the first time you put a leash on her.

lure   To show with your hands or body posture what you want the dog to do.

neutral stimulus Something that has no meaning until it's paired with something either positive or negative.

OFA The Orthopedic Foundation for Animals. The OFA was formed to help breeders address hip dysplasia and other congenital diseases.

opposition reflex The natural reflexive action that makes a dog push or pull against anything that is pushing or pulling against him.

precursor A sign that something is going to happen. This can be a signal that the dog is getting nervous or a sign that something good is going to happen, such as the rattle of a plastic bag, signifying that a dog treat is forthcoming.

Premack Principle The observation that high-probability behavior reinforces low-probability behavior.

provoking stimuli Things your dog may be afraid of, including people, dogs, cows, horses, fence posts, drain pipes, petting in inappropriate ways, the vacuum cleaner—basically anything that makes the dog nervous.

puppy mill A place where dogs of many breeds are bred strictly for money. The bitches are kept in deplorable conditions, the puppies are not socialized, and puppies are taken away from mom and littermates entirely too early. There are no health checks on breeding stock, or on the puppies themselves. "Papers" issued from puppy mills are often fictitious or from unrecognized registries, rendering them useless. Please understand that all the puppies (and kittens) you see at pet shops come from these kinds of places. Yes, they are cute—what puppy isn't cute? Getting a well-adjusted dog from these places is rare, so do your homework!

redirected aggression When a dog (or human) takes an emotion that she can't express in a situation and directs it toward another object, human, or dog.

schedule-induced aggression Inappropriate behavior that arises when the results you get don't match your expectations.

scruff shake   Grabbing the dog by the side of the neck, holding him off the ground, and yelling at him.

socialization   A controlled introduction of various situations and things so that the dog develops positive associations with them.

splitting   (1) Breaking a behavior into many small steps and having the dog master one before going on to the next. (2) When two dogs are playing, a third dog will very often run between them to break up what the dog perceives as play that's too rough. Dogs split from the rear for obvious reasons: there are no teeth in the rear.

stimulus   Any event that affects or is capable of affecting behavior.

stimulus control   The dog responds promptly to a cue in any and all situations, and doesn't respond with the behavior when it isn't asked for.

systematic desensitization   *See* desensitization.

trial   One repetition of a behavior.

variable schedule of reinforcement   When you sometimes give your dog a treat for a correct behavior and don't other times.

Books and Web Resources

These are the books and websites that I recommend the most if you'd like to learn more about positive training and healthier ways to feed your dogs. I firmly believe that diet affects behavior, so I've also included some of my favorite sources addressing those issues as well.

Books

Billinghurst, Ian. *The Barf Diet*. Bathurst, NSW, Australia: Warrigal Publishing, 2001.

———. *Give Your Dog a Bone*. Bathurst, NSW, Australia: Warrigal Publishing, 1993.

———. *Grow Your Pups with Bones*. Bathurst, NSW, Australia: Warrigal Publishing, 1998.

Booth, Sheila. *Purely Positive Training*. Ridgefield, CT: Podium Publications, 1998.

Brown, Kerry, and Wendy Volhard. *Holistic Guide for a Healthy Dog*. New York: Howell Book House, 1995.

Burch, Mary R., and Jon S. Bailey. *How Dogs Learn*. New York: Howell Book House, 1999.

Chance, Paul. *Learning and Behavior*. 4th ed. Pacific Cove, CA: Brooks/Cole, 1999.

Dennison, Pamela S. *Bringing Light to Shadow: A Dog Trainer's Diary.* Wenatchee, WA: Dogwise Publishing, 2005.

———. *Camp R.E.W.A.R.D. for Aggressive Dogs.* Mechanicsburg, PA: Barkleigh Productions, 2005 (video and DVD).

———. *Civilizing the City Dog; A Guide to Rehabilitating Aggressive Dogs in an Urban Environment.* Loveland, CO: Alpine Publications, 2007.

———. *How to Right a Dog Gone Wrong: A Roadmap for Rehabilitating Aggressive Dogs.* Loveland, CO: Alpine Publications, 2005.

———. *Positive Solutions for Standard Behavior Problems.* Mechanicsburg, PA: Barkleigh Productions, 2005 (video and DVD).

———. *The Magic of Shaping: Explore the Possibilities.* Eagle, ID: Tawzer Dog Videos, 2008 (DVD, 4-hour, 2 disks, menu driven, 20+ behaviors).

———. *Training the Whistle Recall.* Belvidere, NJ: Pamela Dennison, 2009 (DVD and whistle, 28 minutes, 5-week program, winner of the Maxwell Award for Best Training Video of 2009 from the Dog Writers Association of America).

Donaldson, Jean. *The Culture Clash.* Berkeley, CA: James and Kenneth Publishers, 1996.

Lorenz, Konrad. *On Aggression.* Translated by Marjorie Latzke. New York: Routledge, 2002.

Pitcairn, Richard H., and Susan Hubble Pitcairn. *Dr. Pitcairn's Complete Guide to Natural Health for Dogs & Cats.* Emmaus, PA: Rodale Press, 1995.

Pryor, Karen. *Don't Shoot the Dog.* Rev. ed. New York: Bantam Books, 1999.

———. *Lads Before the Wind.* Waltham, MA: Sunshine Books, 1994.

Reid, Pamela J. *Excel-erated Learning.* Berkeley, CA: James and Kenneth Publishers, 1996.

Rugaas, Turid. *On Talking Terms with Dogs: Calming Signals.* Wenatchee, WA: Dogwise Publishing, 1997 (book and video).

Sidman, Murray. *Coercion and Its Fallout.* Boston, MA: Authors Cooperative, 1989.

Spector, Morgan. *Clicker Training for Obedience.* Waltham, MA: Sunshine Books, 1999.

Websites for Training and General Dog Issues

These are my favorite websites for training and nutrition. Literally thousands of great sites are on the Internet, but there are also thousands of not-great sites. It takes a while to learn how to separate the wheat from the chaff.

Alternative Veterinary Medicine

www.altvetmed.org

Where to find a holistic veterinarian.

American Kennel Club

www.akc.org

Information about breeds, shows, CGC, and other dog sports.

American Veterinary Society of Animal Behavior

www.avsabonline.org/avsabonline/images/stories/Position_Statements/puppy%20socialization.pdf

www.avsabonline.org/avsabonline/images/stories/Position_Statements/dominance%20statement.pdf

Information about puppy socialization.

Association of Pet Dog Trainers

www.apdt.com

Australian Shepherd Club of America

www.asca.org

Not just for Aussies! They allow any breed as well as mixed breeds to compete in sanctioned trials.

B-Naturals

www.b-naturals.com

Great source for supplements.

Barkleigh Productions Inc.

www.barkleigh.com

Another source for my videos.

Black Ice

www.blackicedogsledding.com

The only source for X-back sledding harnesses—Pam's pick for the best harness for loose-leash walking!

Bluegrace Portuguese Water Dogs

www.bluegrace.com

A source for alternative medicine—not just for Portuguese Water Dogs!

Cambridge Center for Behavioral Studies

www.behavior.org

Great source for information about behavior in lay terms.

Canine Freestyle Federation, Inc.

www.canine-freestyle.org

Information about Canine Freestyle (dancing with your dog).

Canine Water Sports

www.caninewatersports.com

CERF

www.vmdb.org/cerf.htmlClickerSolutions

www.clickersolutions.com

Loads of great information about positive training.

Delta Society

www.deltasociety.org

One of the registries for Therapy Dog work.

Dogwise.com

www.dogwise.com

The place to find all the books and videos/DVDs that are in this listing.

Hearts United for Animals: Puppy Mills

www.hua.org/Prisoners/Puppymills.html

Puppy mill FAQs.

NaturalRearing.com

www.naturalrearing.com

Information on raising your dog the natural way.

North American Dog Agility Council

www.nadac.com

One of the registries for agility.

Orthopedic Foundation for Animals (OFA)

www.offa.org

petswelcome.com

www.petswelcome.com

A listing for hotels that accept pets.

Positive Motivation Dog Training

www.positivedogs.com

My website! Articles, class schedules, and leather tracking harness and whistle training DVD.

Reaching the Animal Mind

www.reachingtheanimalmind.com

Karen Pryor's website. Chock-full of great information.

SitStay

www.sitstay.com

A great source for the books listed here, plus other pet gear.

Stacy's Wag'N'Train

www.wagntrain.com

Super site with fantastic information about training and behavior.

Tawzer Dog Videos

www.tawzerdogvideos.com

A great source for great DVDs—including some of my own.

ThenSome's PetHealth Resource: vaccinations

www.thensome.com/vaccinations.htm

Information about vaccinations and how they really aren't needed as often as veterinarians recommend.

Therapy Dogs International

www.tdi-dog.org

Another registry for Therapy Dog work.

United Kennel Club

www.ukcdogs.com

United States Dog Agility Association

www.usdaa.com

Another registry for agility.

World Canine Freestyle Organization

www.worldcaninefreestyle.org

Another registry for freestyle (dancing with your dog).

Finding a Positive Trainer

So you're hooked on positive training but want some help with the details. There are as many trainers out there with all different levels of expertise and knowledge about learning theory as there are blades of grass. Ask five trainers the best way to train and you'll get 500 different answers. Many trainers think they are positive; they may use a clicker, but they also use a prong collar. This is not positive. This is punishment paired with food.

You'll need to interview your prospective trainer, and these are the questions you should ask:

- How long have you been training?

- What training organizations do you belong to?

- Do you compete in any dog sports? (Not all that important, but I would want to know.)

- What "tools" do you use? (If the answer is prong collars, head halters, and choke collars, run away.)

You can even ask pointed questions such as these:

- If the dog jumps or bites, what would you recommend? (If the answers are in any way violent or hands-on, run away.)

- Can I have references? (Be sure to check them out.)

Ask to observe a few classes. Talk to students after the class. If what you see in the class is disturbing to you, don't join the class. It may take a while and you may have to drive a farther distance than you wanted to, but finding a positive trainer for your best friend will be the best investment you can possibly make.

Index

C

S